Developing Educational Technology
at an Urban Community College

Kate S. Wolfe • Kate Lyons • Carlos Guevara
Editors

Developing Educational Technology at an Urban Community College

Editorial Contributions by Jacqueline DiSanto

Editors
Kate S. Wolfe
Behavioral and Social Sciences
Department
Hostos Community College, CUNY
Bronx, NY, USA

Kate Lyons
Library
Hostos Community College, CUNY
Bronx, NY, USA

Carlos Guevara
Division of Academic Affairs
Hostos Community College, CUNY
Bronx, NY, USA

With Contrib. by
Jacqueline DiSanto
Teacher Education
Hostos Community College
New York, NY, USA

ISBN 978-3-030-17037-0   ISBN 978-3-030-17038-7   (eBook)
https://doi.org/10.1007/978-3-030-17038-7

© The Editor(s) (if applicable) and The Author(s), under exclusive licence to Springer Nature Switzerland AG 2019
This work is subject to copyright. All rights are solely and exclusively licensed by the Publisher, whether the whole or part of the material is concerned, specifically the rights of translation, reprinting, reuse of illustrations, recitation, broadcasting, reproduction on microfilms or in any other physical way, and transmission or information storage and retrieval, electronic adaptation, computer software, or by similar or dissimilar methodology now known or hereafter developed.
The use of general descriptive names, registered names, trademarks, service marks, etc. in this publication does not imply, even in the absence of a specific statement, that such names are exempt from the relevant protective laws and regulations and therefore free for general use.
The publisher, the authors and the editors are safe to assume that the advice and information in this book are believed to be true and accurate at the date of publication. Neither the publisher nor the authors or the editors give a warranty, express or implied, with respect to the material contained herein or for any errors or omissions that may have been made. The publisher remains neutral with regard to jurisdictional claims in published maps and institutional affiliations.

Cover illustration: © Alex Linch / shutterstock.com

This Palgrave Macmillan imprint is published by the registered company Springer Nature Switzerland AG
The registered company address is: Gewerbestrasse 11, 6330 Cham, Switzerland

Foreword

Eugenio María de Hostos Community College is one of seven community colleges within the City University of New York (CUNY) and has been recognized nationally and locally for its technology and innovation. Innovation and change never come easily for institutions of higher education, but they can be accomplished with careful planning, hard work, and patience. Within these pages you will read the strategies used, the obstacles faced, and the research conducted to garner support and to establish a foundation for the effective implementation of change.

Most of the professors at CUNY's community colleges hold doctoral or terminal degrees in their fields, and all are required to conduct research and publish as part of their tenure and promotion process. During the time frame described in this book, the faculty had a twenty-seven-credit hour workload along with the requirements of service and professional growth. As a community college, teaching is vital even though it is only a third of the responsibilities. In Chap. 4, you will hear more about the South Bronx, the location of Hostos. As with most community-college students, Hostos students enter with developmental needs, the majority are first-generation college students, many are parents, and approximately 20% enter with a high-school equivalence in lieu of a high-school diploma. The faculty work hard to support our students in their success, both inside and outside the classroom. Adding technology had to be seen as a support to their teaching and not just another add-on.

There are two separate technology offices on campus, which report to two different divisions. Information Technology is housed within the Division of Administration and Finance and is responsible for the systems on campus. The Office of Instructional Technology (later changed to the Educational Technology Office, or EdTech) reports to the Division of Academic Affairs and focuses on using technology as a pedagogical tool. This was an important distinction that the office first focused on in order to communicate this message. It helped that an opportunity arose to have the director of the EdTech Office take on the additional role of co-director for Hostos' Center for Teaching and Learning. The other co-director is a faculty member. We had prior discussions about the rationale of bringing more synergy between the two offices and reinforcing the connection between technology and pedagogy. When there was an opportunity to restructure some roles, it was a logical choice to make this move. Other benefits include the ability to share resources and not duplicate efforts. Most importantly, it was an important strategy for messaging technology as a pedagogical tool.

Hostos' mission specifically includes technology as a necessary skill for students to have upon graduation to be successful in their careers and further education.

> The mission of Eugenio María de Hostos Community College is to offer access to higher education leading to intellectual growth and socio-economic mobility through the development of linguistic, mathematical, technological, and critical thinking proficiencies needed for lifelong learning and for success in a variety of programs including careers, liberal arts, transfer, and those professional programs leading to licensure.

Technological literacy has also been identified as a required skill by our accrediting body, so technology has a twofold purpose for us. First, these are skills we are committed to teaching our students, and, second, using technology can have positive outcomes in the teaching and learning process.

It was critical for the faculty to understand that technology is not just the latest gadget but that it is there to support, enhance, and sometimes supplement teaching. A great example of this is in Chap. 6, which explains the iPad initiative. When iPads were first introduced on campus, there were faculty who were interested in class sets due to the novelty, but without professional development regarding the pedagogical benefits and structure to guide their use, the full benefits of the tool would not have been realized. Wanting to use the latest gadgets, and in this case technologies, without fully thinking through pedagogical purposes is one challenge that the EdTech Office had to address. On the other end of the continuum, EdTech also faced challenges when confronted with data-driven skeptics of new initiatives. As you will read in Chaps. 6 and 16, Hostos faculty and staff took the time to collect data and implement research studies to determine the effectiveness of various technologies, in part to share with their colleagues but also to validate that using these technologies is having a positive impact on student learning. In between the two ends of the continuum are faculty who are intrigued by the technologies but uncomfortable taking the perceived risks of using the technologies. The faculty are accustomed to being the expert in the classroom. They know their discipline better than anyone else on campus, and therefore, they are comfortable being able to address anything that may arise in class. Using a new technology, especially in front of an audience of students, presents a number of variables that could go wrong and could cause more than one moment of awkwardness and uncertainty in the classroom. In my opinion, this is actually good for students to witness. We ask them to be vulnerable in the learning process every day and yet the role models they see are faculty, who appear to know everything and never struggle with learning. Yet, we all know learning is hard and messy. Letting students watch us struggle with the process not only lets them know this is not just acceptable but also normal, and it is also an opportunity for students to see how we move through the learning process. Getting to this point, however, requires supporting the faculty as they take risks and helping them understand the role of the Office of Educational Technology in providing a safety net.

Change rarely occurs by happenstance. The faculty and staff at Hostos share their strategies, structures, and struggles in the pages of this book. The strategies and structures can be replicated and adapted to fit the culture of your own campus. Sharing the struggles and lessons learned goes back to my concept that learning is hard and messy but is also part of the process. We definitely learned much through these changes, we took risks, and we took time to stop and reflect and adjust as necessary. We also adjusted the incentives as we went along. At the beginning, with grant funds, it was easier to be more generous with release time and stipends, but as the culture shifted and the funding waned, we were able to implement less expensive strategies, such as having one mentor for several faculty instead of the original one-on-one mentoring model that was used initially.

The authors of these chapters are Hostos' innovators, risk-takers, and cheerleaders. Not only were they willing to try new technologies, they wanted to bring others along with them. They are just a few of Hostos' 187 full-time and 350 part-time faculty. Together they became the current to move the culture of the institution. I hope you enjoy reading about their journeys and see how you can create your own.

Hostos Community College, CUNY Christine Mangino
Bronx, NY, USA

Contents

Section I Our Context and Why It Matters   1

1 **Introduction**   3
Carlos Guevara, Kate Lyons, and Kate S. Wolfe

2 **Leading Above the Fray: Turning Challenges into Opportunities**   11
Carlos Guevara

3 **Change Management in Practice: Creating a Culture That Promotes Technology Adoption**   21
Carlos Guevara, Kate Lyons, and Kate S. Wolfe

4 **Who We Are and Why It Matters**   35
Elys Vasquez-Iscan

5 **Where We Fit**   51
Kristopher Bryan Burrell

Section II   A Mindful Approach to Community Building — 63

6   Inspiring the Innovators Through Professional Development Initiatives — 65
Carlos Guevara, Wilfredo Rodriguez, and David Dos Santos

7   The Online Learning Initiative: Training the Early Adopters — 79
Jacqueline M. DiSanto and Carlos Guevara

8   Reaching Beyond the Innovators — 95
Kate S. Wolfe

9   Celebrating the Innovators — 105
Kate Lyons

10   Through the Eyes of an Early Adopter — 119
Amy J. Ramson

Section III   Opportunities and Challenges — 123

11   Preparing Our Students — 125
George J. Rosa, David Dos Santos, and Carlos Guevara

12   Expanding Access to Education Through Open Educational Resources (OERs) — 135
Lisa Tappeiner, Jacqueline M. DiSanto, and Kate Lyons

13   Creating a Safe Environment for Innovators — 147
Lisa Tappeiner, Kate Lyons, Sandy Figueroa, and Linda Ridley

Section IV "I only work with the converted": Converting the Technology Skeptics Through Proof and Credibility ... 161

14 Living with the Skeptics: A Personal Journey ... 163
Sandy Figueroa

15 Connecting the Dots: Data from a Personal Perspective ... 169
Kate S. Wolfe

16 Building Community Through Assessment ... 173
Kate S. Wolfe and Jacqueline M. DiSanto

17 Moving Through Hostos, a Student Grown into a Staff and Faculty Member ... 197
Rocio Rayo

Afterword ... 203

Index ... 207

NOTES ON CONTRIBUTORS

Kristopher Bryan Burrell PhD, is Assistant Professor of History at Hostos Community College. Burrell got his doctorate in US History from the CUNY Graduate Center in 2011. His research interests include the civil rights movement in New York City and twentieth-century African American intellectual history. Burrell's work has been published in the *Western Journal of Black Studies* (Spring 2012), and his essays have appeared in the online forums *Public Seminar* and *The Gotham Center for New York City History* in 2018. He has written a chapter that will appear in *The Strange Careers of the Jim Crow North: Segregation and Struggle Outside of the South* (2019). Burrell is also coordinator of the Hostos Online Learning Assessment Task Force and his pedagogical work about online learning has appeared in the *Hispanic Educational Technology Services Online Journal* (April 2016). He is working on a book manuscript titled, *Outsmarting Racism: New York's Black Intellectuals and Theorizing Northern Racism, 1945–1968*.

Jacqueline M. DiSanto EdD, is Associate Professor of Education at Hostos Community College/CUNY and Coordinator of Early-Childhood Education. Her areas of expertise include curriculum, administration and supervision, online learning, and open-educational resources. She is founding member of the Peer Observation Improvement Network for Teaching; she serves on the Instructional Evaluation and Hostos Online Learning Assessment committees. Two of her recent works focused on student perceptions of online learning and on assessment that addressed measuring skills development through general-education competencies and program-learning outcomes. She is vice chair of the Board of Trustees of the New York City Montessori Charter School.

Sandy Figueroa is an associate professor and coordinator of the Office Technology Unit in the Business Department of Eugenio Maria de Hostos Community College (CUNY). She received both her bachelor's degree and master's degree in Business Education from Hunter College. Figueroa has taught both asynchronous and hybrid courses since 1995. She has chaired and served on a number of committees at the college.

Carlos Guevara has worked at Hostos Community College for over 20 years, and has over 15 years of experience in educational technology. Guevara is the Director of the Office of Educational Technology, and Co-Director of the Center for Teaching and Learning and his main role is to provide vision to the Institution in bringing innovation to teaching and learning through the effective use of technology. Guevara has established a successful organizational culture shift around technology adoption, implementing initiatives centered on mentoring and communities of practice. He has presented a variety of academic technology topics in several national and international conferences, and received several recognitions for his work. His main research areas of interest are online learning, faculty development, and organizational culture change in higher education. Guevara has served as Chair of the CUNY Centers for Teaching and Learning Advisory Council, and Chair of the Hostos HEO Organization. Carlos holds a BS and Master's degrees in Computer Science and is pursuing his doctorate degree in Educational Technology at Teachers College, Columbia University.

Kate Lyons is an associate professor in the library at Hostos Community College of CUNY. She is head of Reference and Technology at the library, and also is Communities of Practice Coordinator for the Office of Educational Technology at Hostos. She is interested in organizational behavior and change management, and also in educational and library technology. She holds a Master of Science in Management from the Wagner School of Public Service at NYU, a Master of Science in Library and Information Science from the University of Illinois at Urbana-Champaign, and a Bachelor of Arts degree in English from Grinnell College.

Iber Poma is a student services coordinator of the Office of Educational Technology at Eugenio Maria de Hostos Community College (CUNY). He received a Bachelor of Computer Science from Hunter College. He leads the iPad in the Classroom and Panopto Lecture Capture initiatives.

Amy J. Ramson is a professor at Hostos Community College (CUNY) in the Bronx, New York, where she has taught in the Public Policy and Law Unit since 1990. She is an attorney licensed to practice in New York State and Georgia since 1983 and 1987, respectively, and practices in the areas of immigration and international law. She has practiced at large and boutique law firms in New York City and at an international law firm in Geneva. Her areas of academic research are sexual harassment education, instructional technology, and service-learning. Most recently, she is a founding member of her college's service-learning committee and has written an editor's choice article on sexual harassment. Her peer-reviewed manuscripts and numerous conference presentations have focused on the benefits and assessment of service-learning. She is a member of the newly formed campus subcommittee on collaborative online international learning (COIL) and is piloting COIL in Fall 2019.

Rocio Rayo serves as the liaison between Hostos Lincoln Academy of Science and Hostos Community College (CUNY) in the Bronx, New York. She manages an Early College Initiative where students graduate from high-school with both their AA and HS Diplomas. She graduated from Hostos Community College in 2011 and completed her BA and MA in History at the City College of New York in 2014. Her thesis focused on re-imaging the "failed feminist agenda" narrative that emerged from second wave feminist historians who studied the Sandinista Revolution with third wave feminist intellectual tools that incorporated stories of state sanctioned reproductive health initiatives. She began adjuncting at Hostos in 2014 and transitioned into her current position as a higher education officer in 2017.

Linda Ridley is a lecturer at CUNY's Hostos Community College, where she teaches introductory business and management, both face-to-face and online. Her research interests are organizational development and global diversity, which she teaches at the graduate level at CUNY's School of Professional Studies. Ridley, who has been designated as an Expert Consultant by the Asian Productivity Organization out of Tokyo,

Japan, uses her expertise in global business and change management to provide a unique perspective on the innovative challenges presented by online learning. She is a member of the newly formed campus subcommittee on collaborative online international learning. Ridley was selected as one of 18 faculty worldwide by The Case Centre at London's Cranfield University for a scholarship to author a business case study based on one of her publications. Additionally her articles have been published in the peer-reviewed *Journal of Higher Education Theory and Practice*. Ridley attended Virginia Commonwealth University, and earned her Master of Business Administration from the Mason School of Business at the College of William and Mary, Williamsburg, Virginia. She is currently pursuing a doctorate in Educational Leadership at St. John's University, Queens, New York.

Wilfredo Rodriguez is coordinator at the office of Educational Technology since April 2012 and has held varied positions at the college. He oversees the daily operations of the office by making sure all academic year goals are clearly delineated and accomplished in the best possible way. Additionally, he supervises and implements many different projects. Rodriguez began as an ESL/Spanish tutor in 2002 in the Coordinated Freshman Program (CFP). After working for two years in CFP and also facilitating writing workshops, he began working as an administrative assistance in 2004 for the Title V Grant with Prof. Kim Sanabria as the Principal Investigator. When the grant expired, he went to work for the Office of Academic Affairs as a HEO where he undertook various responsibilities. Rodriguez holds a MS and BS in Computer Science from Lehman College. After graduating, he has continuously kept updating his knowledge in the field by researching the newest technology and how it adapted to education. He has been programming in Asp.net MVC framework for a couple of years and has developed many applications and supported many others that he inherited when the programmers left Educational Technology.

George J. Rosa has Bachelor degrees in Biology and Media Arts and Masters in Biology and Science Education. He has been a part of Hostos EdTech since 2002, where he is senior instructional designer and campus Blackboard Administrator. In all he has over 20 years of experience in educational technology, educational media design, and distance learning working at Hostos and CUNY as well as for private industry and non-profits, including as a developer and editor of digital and hard-copy products for such clients as John Wiley & Sons, Merck & Co., Prudential Insurance, *The New York Times*, and Human Relations Media, and as an author of teacher guides and lesson plans for the PBS Nature series. Rosa is also an adjunct instructor of Biology and has developed and taught online Introductory Biology and Anatomy and Physiology courses at Hostos and has many years of experience teaching Biology as well as Painting and Drawing at the college and secondary school levels.

David Dos Santos is an instructional designer in the Office of Educational Technology at Hostos Community College of CUNY. He serves as the ePortfolio Administrator and is one of the lead developers of the "Are You Ready?" online readiness course at Hostos. Dos Santos has over a decade of experience in Educational Technology and continues to explore methods to implement new technology into the classroom every day. He holds a Bachelor of Arts degree in Emerging Media from Hunter College.

Lisa Tappeiner is an associate professor in the library at Hostos Community College of CUNY. She is the library's Head of Technical Services and Collection Development, and is also an instructor of the college's First Year Seminar. She is interested in reading practices of college students and integrating open and primary resources into teaching. She previously worked at Fordham University. She holds a Masters of Arts in Comparative Literature and Library and Information Studies from the University of Wisconsin, Madison, and a Bachelor of Arts in French and History from the University of Minnesota, Twin Cities.

Elys Vasquez-Iscan is an assistant professor at Hostos Community College of CUNY where she holds a dual appointment in the Health Education Unit and the Aging and Health Unit. She holds a master's degree of public health (MPH) from New York University and a doctorate degree in Health Education from Teachers College, Columbia University. She teaches several hybrid and asynchronous health courses. Her research focuses on the utilization of e-health to address health inequities, HIV prevention strategies among college students, and addressing the digital gap in underserved urban communities. She has been the recipient of an ELEVATE Fellowship from the University of Pennsylvania and a Fulbright Fellowship. She was the collaborator of a multisectoral grant from the Aetna Foundation to make the South Bronx a healthy beverage zone. She has taught a diverse student population including students in the prison to college pipeline program at the New York State Otisville Correctional Facility. As part of her efforts to promote health and health careers to underserved populations, she mentors a vast amount of ethnic and racial minority college students, particularly doctoral students during the dissertation process.

Kate S. Wolfe PhD, is Assistant Professor of Psychology in the Behavioral and Social Sciences Department at Hostos Community College, the City University of New York (CUNY). Wolfe is a social psychologist with research interests in quantitative reasoning among urban community college students, student perceptions of online learning, using iPads in teaching, and urban college student attitudes toward sexual minorities. She joined the planning committee for the Project for Relevant and Improved Mathematics Education, funded by the Teagle Foundation in 2015. She is the Principal Investigator for the ongoing Hostos Online Learning Assessment project that began in Fall 2015. She has been a visiting scholar at Teachers College, Columbia University, as a fellow of the Metropolitan Colleges Institute for Teaching Improvement, a program that focuses on the nature of a liberal education at urban colleges.

List of Figures

Fig. 3.1	Innovations Web	28
Fig. 7.1	Growth in asynchronous courses	89
Fig. 7.2	Growth in hybrid courses	90
Fig. 7.3	Growth in percentage of hybrid and asynchronous offerings	91
Fig. 8.1	Student perceptions of online learning – Spring 2018 data	101

SECTION I

Our Context and Why It Matters

CHAPTER 1

Introduction

Carlos Guevara, Kate Lyons, and Kate S. Wolfe

In 2010, education experienced a proliferation of mobile learning through iPads, smartphones, and laptop computers, and the popularization of massive open online courses (MOOCs) was a catalyst for more widespread acceptance of online learning. At the same time, during a period of transition in Hostos Community College's leadership, Provost Carmen Coballes-Vega and Associate Dean Christine Mangino asked Carlos Guevara to be the interim director of the Office of Educational Technology (EdTech). In his new role, Guevara became responsible for a formidable task in the college's strategic plan: an across-the-board increase in the use of educational technology on campus and, especially, an increase in the number of faculty members who use Blackboard to 100%.

C. Guevara (✉)
Division of Academic Affairs, Hostos Community College, CUNY,
Bronx, NY, USA
e-mail: cguevara@hostos.cuny.edu

K. Lyons
Library, Hostos Community College, CUNY, Bronx, NY, USA
e-mail: clyons@hostos.cuny.edu

K. S. Wolfe
Behavioral and Social Sciences Department, Hostos Community College,
CUNY, Bronx, NY, USA
e-mail: kwolfe@hostos.cuny.edu

© The Author(s) 2019
K. S. Wolfe et al. (eds.), *Developing Educational Technology at an Urban Community College*, https://doi.org/10.1007/978-3-030-17038-7_1

In appointing Guevara to this position, they put the office into the hands of a different type of manager than had been there. Management literature recognizes a type of leader who is not a stabilizing status quo manager, but is instead a change agent. One reference source explains, "In simple terms, change agents are the individuals or groups that undertake the task of initiating and managing change in a company" ("Change Agent Roles and Skills", 2013, p. 50). While managers keep projects, tasks, people, and resources moving, change agents make organizations switch directions. In order to fulfill the objective set by the provost and associate dean, Guevara and his team would need to change the way many faculty members at Hostos thought about teaching with technology. This book focuses on the decade of change and the teams and initiatives that formed after 2010. This chapter begins with the formation of the EdTech team—the core team that includes Guevara, the faculty liaisons, and the EdTech office staff, and introduces their strategies for meeting their technology adoption goals.

Background: Quantifying Technology Adoption Success

Hostos Community College is a small college in the South Bronx, part of the City University of New York (CUNY). CUNY is a system of 11 senior colleges; 7 community colleges; and 6 graduate, honors, and professional schools serving over 275,000 students in the New York City area (CUNY, 2019). Hostos is a Hispanic-Serving Institution that primarily educates underserved, underrepresented students. Hostos students are mostly female, Hispanic and African-American, first generation, full-time, and more often than not in need of remediation (Hostos Community College/OIRSA, 2018) (see Chap. 4). Despite the challenges that Hostos students face, and the challenges that Hostos faculty and staff face, and working without the resources afforded at private colleges, the EdTech team saw a resounding success in meeting the technology adoption goals.

Over almost a decade, the number of course sections offered online has more than quadrupled (fall and spring semesters combined, including both hybrid and asynchronous courses), from 50 in 2010 to 231 in 2018. The number of hybrid courses almost doubled, increasing from 37 in fall 2012 to 73 courses offered in fall 2018. Additionally, the number of asynchronous or fully online courses more than doubled, increasing from 18 in fall 2012 to 50 courses offered in fall 2018. Currently, nearly 78% of faculty have activated their Blackboard courses, up from 25% in 2010. Given that educational institutions tend to be steeped in tradition and often have byzantine paths of communication among departments, offices, and the different layers of faculty and staff, this level of technology adoption is laudable. By 2018, technology had clearly permeated multiple departments, from Humanities to Behavioral and Social Sciences, Natural Sciences, Math, English, Language and Cognition, and Education. Educational Technology has seen an increase in use by all members of the Hostos community—faculty, staff, and students. Faculty members are taking risks to use new hardware, software, and approaches in their pedagogy and their research. Additionally, while the number of full-time staff members in the EdTech office has remained consistent at approximately seven staff members, the office has increased the number of faculty members working as faculty liaisons and in other roles that offer release time from their regular duties to focus on projects for the office. Hostos also collaborates actively with other CUNY campuses, such as Lehman College, Bronx Community College, and John Jay College on educational technology projects and has received several awards for these collaborations.

Background: Guevara and His Immediate Predecessors

Guevara, who describes his background and leadership strategy in more depth in Chap. 2, managed the EdTech office through the decade of change that began in 2010. His story is especially relevant to Hostos, as he began his career as a student at Hostos after arriving in the United States from Ecuador. He completed his bachelor's degree at City College (CUNY), and his first full-time job was in the Office of Educational Technology at Hostos. Guevara's background is representative of how many of our students come to this college. His transition from Hostos student to his first position at Hostos, in Educational Technology, was a formative moment for him as it began a history of nimbleness with work expectations and a background with a flexible, emerging field that would require constant learning. The way he learned to be adaptable, and his willingness to see challenges and struggles as opportunities to think outside the box for an innovative solution, gave him the background to be open to innovation, willing to take risks, and taught him the mind-set needed to succeed.

In order to meet the objectives set by the provost and associate dean, Guevara and his team would need to change the way faculty members at Hostos thought about teaching with technology. The team considered their values and the values they wanted to espouse, and they recognized that the technology adoption they needed to see would depend, at least in part, on encouraging the organizational culture to align with the EdTech team's culture. The foundation for creating this change was well established. Previous directors of the Office of Educational Technology had been full-time, tenured faculty members who were released from teaching to manage the office. The most recent director had stepped down to go back to teaching, and the EdTech office had recently reopened (fall 2010) after a more modern renovation of the space, making it more conducive to group interaction and collaborative practices. For Guevara, who had been a staff member in the EdTech office since its creation, his appointment to the position of director was a promotion, but, most importantly, it was also an opportunity for him and all the faculty and staff members working with EdTech to reassess the office's programs and structures and propose and implement forward-thinking modifications.

Forming the Team: Appointing the First Faculty Liaison

Appointing Guevara as interim director was a pivotal moment as he and the EdTech team galvanized a shift in the way educational technology fit into the college's culture. While most of the EdTech staff remained in place after this initial moment of change and stayed relatively stable over the decade that followed, there was a reorganization of roles, as well as the creation of faculty liaison as a job title.

Along with her appointment of Guevara to the director position, the provost and associate dean asked Professor Kate Lyons, a reference and technology librarian who served on EdTech's Committee on Academic Computing, to be released part-time from her duties in the library to be a faculty liaison to EdTech. The role of faculty liaison began as a way to help build a community of practice around online-course development, as well as meet this daunting goal of 100% of faculty using Blackboard. Because the office was previously led by a faculty member and because faculty members have specific concerns in terms of promotion and tenure, having the faculty perspective on EdTech initiatives provided a much-needed and balanced viewpoint for the office. CUNY librarians have faculty status, sharing the same requirements for promotion and tenure as teaching faculty. Librarians, however, are on a 12-month contract and work regular

35-hour work weeks. Thus, librarians tend to straddle well the work culture of teaching faculty and full-time staff.

Guevara and Lyons, realizing that they were looking at the need for organizational culture change, sought out management literature to determine how to encourage technology adoption by faculty at Hostos and at the same time promote innovation and risk-taking. They prioritized establishing a culture of collaboration and innovation, and researched how ideas are spread, focusing primarily on the diffusion of innovation theory, which explains how, when, and why new ideas are adopted in an organization (Rogers, 2003), as well as theories about organizational change. Their goal was to mindfully plan initiatives and to create teams that would infuse educational technology across the curriculum at Hostos. They wanted to select management theories to guide their planning and match Hostos' organizational culture. Upon reflection a decade later, Guevara's leadership encouraged those who worked with EdTech to cultivate a culture of risk-taking, innovation, and collaboration. Looking back over the last ten years, Guevara turned out to be the change agent that EdTech needed at that time—one who would inspire a culture of risk-taking and collaboration.

Initial Challenges: Communication, Consistency, and Sustainability

Technology adoption and culture change at Hostos are challenging because of the difficulty communication can pose in a large organization and also because of a lack of administrative consistency among all of the college's divisions and departments. More than half of the course sections are taught by adjunct faculty members at Hostos. Because adjunct faculty are not on campus as often and are less likely to attend campus-wide committees and meetings than full-time faculty, communication with that group can be especially challenging. While adjunct faculty may read email and written memos, they are often engaged for far fewer hours each week than full-time faculty, and their focus is more on teaching than on research or becoming a part of the campus culture. Additionally, each academic department has a different way of encouraging compliance with Blackboard use. Adjunct faculty, as well as full-time faculty who engage in projects or teach with faculty on other campuses, might have challenges stepping from one organizational culture to another, even within the same CUNY system. Another significant challenge in many higher education institutions is the lack of structure for the support and sustainability of projects. A short-term planning mentality can end up terminating or abandoning promising initiatives that only start showing results once the funding runs out. Hostos' EdTech experienced that as well, and funding has itself proven to be challenging.

Expanding the Core Team: Appointing New Faculty Liaisons

In 2015, after analyzing the progress on the different fronts, Guevara needed to create a systematic structure to promote communities of practice and reward risk-taking and innovation; therefore, EdTech decided to reimagine the role of the faculty liaisons to help build this structure. As the position's responsibilities grew with the office, the position split in two. Lyons took on the role of Coordinator of Community of Practice, with the objective of encouraging faculty members to try new things and at the same time keep the momentum going among those early adopters. The Coordinator of Online Learning Assessment position was created to more intentionally assess the initiatives and the approach to developing and delivering online teaching at Hostos. This position had a heavy focus on researching faculty and student perceptions to inform EdTech about necessary enhancements to its initiatives and approaches. Dr. Kate Wolfe, Assistant Professor of Psychology, was appointed as this second faculty liaison for the office. Woven through both faculty liaison roles was the underlying focus on outreach, community building, assessment of the different EdTech initiatives, and dissemination of research. In 2018, Dr. Kristopher Burrell, Assistant Professor of History, became a third liaison to EdTech.

Managing the EdTech Budget

The EdTech team has received support from administration, who believed in the importance of identifying and providing funding to accomplish the goals of infusing technology into teaching and learning at the college. Initially, when the EdTech office was created in 2002, funding for the three instructional designers and resources came from three different grants. As that investment was increasingly proving itself worthwhile, the administration then provided funding for a coordinator and a college lab-technician to provide additional support. During the first decade of the office's existence, a similar personnel and funding structure was kept, and the dependency from grants remained. One of the first priorities for Guevara was to advocate for the institutionalization of the office's operating budget, which would provide stability for the staff and would support the initiatives and activities carried out by the office. The EdTech team is currently comprised of the director, three faculty liaisons, the office's coordinator, the coordinator of student support, coordinator of online learning, three full-time and two part-time instructional designers, two part-time technical support assistants, and between three to five instructional design interns. The operational budget is funded by Hostos, student technology fees, and grants.

Future Chapters: An Assemblage of the Hostos Voices That Enabled Success

Status quo managers have a crucial role in organizations—stabilizing and providing day-to-day management. However, change agents are a different sort of managers. The process of organizational change has been known to be a huge undertaking and difficult to accomplish. Convincing groups to learn new ways of working and, in the case of educational technology, shifting the way they teach is challenging to say the least. Although theories of education have evolved over the decades, until recently with the advent of new and more robust communication technologies and with the exception of correspondence courses, most credit-bearing education has taken place in person. Substituting online components for class time can feel like taking the teacher out of the equation, though that is far from the truth. Teachers also tend to have strong feelings about the effectiveness or shortcomings of their own face-to-face education, which may have influenced their decision to become teachers. Leading through change requires a manager who understands the way faculty members and staff feel about change.

According to Kotter, "People change what they do less because they are given analysis that shifts their thinking than because they are shown a truth that influences their feelings" (2002, p. 1). Change has an inherent emotional component that must be addressed. Hence, we often tend to change minor elements that seldom have deeper influence rather than change the culture of an organization. Finding out how to enable the members of an organization to identify those feeling influencers is key to initiating change. Focusing only on the cognitive aspect—shifting thought processes—will not ultimately result in real change.

Although the following chapters in this book focus on the decade of change and the teams that formed after 2010, the college was quite actively involved in educational technology before that year. The structure that already existed, upon which the changes from 2010 until the present were built, was crucial for the successes of the Office of Educational Technology. As such, Guevara began to manage through this period of rapid change, remaining cognizant of the organization's current structure and its history of planning and short-term initiatives, and trying to work with the challenges and opportunities provided by those structures.

References

Change Agent Roles and Skills. (2013). In M. H. Ferrara (Ed.), *Gale business insights handbook of cultural transformation* (pp. 47–56). Detroit, MI: Gale. Retrieved from http://link.galegroup.com.hostos.ezproxy.cuny.edu/apps/doc/CX2759200012/GVRL?u=cuny_bron60695&sid=GVRL&xid=4a52f7be

Hostos Community College, Office of Institutional Research and Student Assessment (HCC OIRSA). (2018). *Hostos Community College: Student profile.* Retrieved from http://www.hostos.cuny.edu/Hostos/media/Office-of-the-President/Institutional-Research-Assessment/Profile-thru-S16.pdf

Kotter, J. P. (2002). *The heart of change.* Boston: Harvard Business School Publishing.

Rogers, E. M. (2003). *Diffusion of innovations* (5th ed.). New York: Simon and Schuster.

The City University of New York. (2019). *CUNY colleges & schools.* Retrieved from http://www2.cuny.edu/about/colleges-schools

CHAPTER 2

Leading Above the Fray: Turning Challenges into Opportunities

Carlos Guevara

I recently read these words of wisdom—"Bridging the gap between what is happening and what is possible is what change management is all about" (Pascale & Sternin, 2005). From the very beginning, I've always considered it my responsibility to be a connector—someone who builds bridges between parts of an organization and between people, between now and the future we collectively can imagine. I remember the day I accepted my first professional position in educational technology at Hostos like it was yesterday. The year was 2002, and I was a newly minted computer science graduate full of enthusiasm and ready to take on the world, and, at the same time, full of the trepidation and uncertainty about embarking on a new career. It was a new position in a then-emerging field called Instructional Design. In those days, there were no standards or best practices for instructional designers, and even educational technologists weren't always in agreement about our roles and responsibilities. As I was leaving the office of the director of the Office of Educational Technology, my new boss and former teacher, I ran into one of my new colleagues, an experienced instructor and media

C. Guevara (✉)
Division of Academic Affairs, Hostos Community College, CUNY, Bronx, NY, USA
e-mail: cguevara@hostos.cuny.edu

© The Author(s) 2019
K. S. Wolfe et al. (eds.), *Developing Educational Technology at an Urban Community College*, https://doi.org/10.1007/978-3-030-17038-7_2

designer. After greeting me warmly, he asked me what my new job entailed. I remained speechless for what seemed like minutes, although probably just a few seconds, thinking about this question: What does it actually mean to be a professional instructional designer? My response was vague. I shared my educational background in Computer Science and Programming. But pondering over that question, I began to realize, and know even more firmly now, that whatever my job description, my role as an instructional designer would require me to evolve and continue to grow, and that, because I worked in an emerging field, it was up to me to create a professional path for myself. From the very first day, I knew I wanted to use my skills and education in ways that would positively impact my colleagues, my university, and my society. That question—what does my job entail?—continues to motivate me as I build the expertise that seemed elusive when I started this journey. In this ever evolving field of educational technology, I know I need to be constantly learning, not only about technology, but also about how it affects people and their environments. Recognizing the constant need to evolve drives my tendency to be a change agent, to encourage professional growth among members of my team, and to constantly look for new ways to do our part in fulfilling the college's mission.

Now, in 2019, I am the director of the Office of Educational Technology and co-director of the Center for Teaching and Learning at Hostos. After more than 17 years of experience in Educational Technology, I see my role as providing vision on how to embrace innovation through the integration of technology and pedagogy to improve student success. My role is also to identify and establish effective practices for creating a culture of continuous improvement and innovation in teaching and learning. I believe that, in order to carry out a successful initiative, whether on a small or large scale, it is important to account for the human element of the team and the members of the organization. Each member of a team is important and each plays a crucial role in motivating the members of the organization to take an active role in this culture of risk-taking and innovation.

The need to adapt and to embrace change has been a constant throughout my life. When I emigrated to New York City from Ecuador, I had to reinvent myself quickly to continue my university education. Living in New York, one of the most diverse cities and most expensive in the world, made my reinvention more challenging but at the same time more rewarding. Being bilingual and working in a community college which is also an Hispanic-serving institution has enabled me to understand the specific challenges experienced by many students and faculty who are learning about new technology for the first time and has led me to consider how educational technology represents an opportunity to our bilingual students. My perspective is also informed by the many positions I have held at Hostos since 1998. Having been a student, tutor, instructional designer, adjunct instructor, coordinator, and now director has given me a broad range of experiences, which has informed my work in EdTech and helped fulfill what I envisioned the first day I started working at EdTech in 2002.

In the past 15 years, Hostos has made great strides in educational innovation and adopting technologies that enhance the ways we teach our students in the classroom and online. We were recognized as the nation's leading digital community college by the Center for Digital Education in 2016. We ranked second in 2018 and we were among the top five in previous years. My EdTech team has received several CUNY Excellence in Technology awards for the many projects and initiatives developed over the years, and we received the International Blackboard Catalyst Award for Optimizing the Student Experience in 2017. I feel very proud to have contributed to our college's success.

Learning is a continuous process, and we must be open to different perspectives to embrace our differences, and thus be able to serve as agents of change in our community. Obtaining different perspectives beyond the professional development opportunities offered at my college has been the determining factor in my advancement. Attending leadership training and researching leadership and organizational change has enabled me to broaden my frames of reference and see challenges from different angles. Putting on the hat of a lifelong learner and establishing and engaging with different networks of professionals inside and outside the field has been crucial. I keep up with organizations such as Educause, Online Learning Consortium, Professional and Organizational Development (POD) Network, International Society for Technology in Education (ISTE), National Institute for Staff and Organizational Development (NISOD), and the American Association of Colleges and Universities (AACU), to name a few.

How Did I Become an Educational Technologist?

Coming from a humble family in an urban area in Ecuador, one of the most important lessons I learned early in life was that a lack of resources doesn't have to be an obstacle. My grandmother, Rosa Sánchez, is one of my heroes. Despite all the challenges she had to face in her life—not knowing how to read, having to raise her seven children alone due to the early departure of my grandfather, having to work in the fields and crops to provide a better future for her children—she instilled in me the greatest values and motivations that I always carry with me. She taught me perseverance, clear purpose, resourcefulness, and to have passion for what you believe in and want to achieve in life. These lessons have always been present in the journey of my life and have helped me overcome the obstacles and barriers I have faced to achieve my personal, educational, and professional goals.

I came to this country when I was 20 years old, after graduating from high school and serving for a year in the army in Ecuador. I came with the clear goal of completing a university education and becoming a professional in the field of technology. I had to learn to live with a new family, adapt to a new culture, and speak a new language, as quickly as possible in order to start college. I learned English through different educational programs, and I also chose jobs that forced me to interact with people in my new language. A few months after my arrival in New York, I enrolled at the City University of New York (CUNY) and was accepted at Hostos Community College where I worked as a tutor in Mathematics and later as a tutor in Economics and Computer Science. In my constant search for opportunities to learn and practice the language, these jobs helped me enormously to improve my skills and at the same time to learn about the student culture and their needs in higher education.

I transferred to the City College of New York to get my degree in Computer Science, but I never lost contact with Hostos. I continued working as a tutor until I finished my undergraduate education. In 2002, just as I was completing my undergraduate degree, my former Mathematics professor, Dr. Loreto Porte, who at that time was the director of the Office of Instructional Technology, invited me to join the team and work as a multimedia specialist. My answer was an immediate "yes." I was at the forefront of the perfect opportunity for developing my knowledge and contributing to this new office at Hostos. A team of three multimedia specialists, with guidance and leadership from the director, began a journey to formalize ad hoc initiatives that had been initiated by the faculty but until then had lacked the institutional support necessary to succeed and expand. The technology back then had many limitations compared to what is possible today; however, we had the opportunity to introduce state-of-the-art technology at that time and develop applications with interactive and adaptive-learning concepts in mind. My experience in computer science and the engineering and design background of the other team members were useful for developing many applications and online websites for disciplines such as Developmental Mathematics, Health Education, and Sociology to support faculty using technology to improve their teaching.

Hostos was one of the first colleges in the CUNY system to establish an office dedicated to academic technology assistance, and to offer faculty a space for professional development and the exploration of new technologies. The office was fortunate to have a full-time director, who was able to establish a solid foundation to help faculty explore ways to integrate technology into their teaching.

In 2008, there was a change in administration at Hostos Community College: both the president and provost left the office within a year of each other, and most administrators of the Office of Academic Affairs also changed. During that transition period, the Office of Instructional Technology, which until that time was led by a faculty member with full-time release of teaching responsibilities, also changed their leadership. A different faculty member with only partial release from teaching responsibilities was chosen to run the office. This change in release-time distribution created a greater workload and increased responsibilities for the coordinator. Although the new director, Dr. Carl Grindley, stayed only for a few semesters, his leadership approach was completely opposite to that of the previous director and he left a lasting impact on the way the team functioned. He encouraged the coordinators and multimedia specialists to be more visible and connect more directly with faculty. A transition period followed for a couple of semesters and, although I managed the office unofficially during that period, I was appointed as the new director in 2012.

Reflections from This Period of Change

Administrative restructuring is very common in higher education and can lead to instability, lack of continuity of initiatives, and a cumulative delay in the adoption of technology and innovation. However, I always like to use the phrase "for every challenge, there is always an opportunity," and the challenge of providing stability to an office that went through a long period of change provided the opportunity to create an exercise to visualize a culture of innovation and organizational change. As a student, tutor, instructional designer, and in my other roles at Hostos and CUNY, I had the opportunity to observe and learn from the diversity of cultures, mentalities, and expectations of the individuals with whom I came into contact. The different types of leadership styles of my previous supervisors and the various roles they played in shaping the culture of the organization with respect to the academic use of technology made me who I am today.

The creation of the Committee of Information Learning Commons (ILC) in 2007 opened my eyes to the potential of organizational change and how I could play a positive role in the betterment of organizations. The committee's mission was to increase the services of existing and independently managed technology-related services by connecting them to each other through a virtual commons that transcended physical spaces and departmental divisions. EdTech, the Library, the Academic Computing Center (the computer lab for students), Information Technology, and Career Services worked together to establish a virtual-commons space to provide students with a seamless experience regardless of where they go to get support (Elsayed et al., 2013). Although the ILC Committee became inactive in 2014, it provided a solid basis for continuing to cultivate partnerships between departments on campus. The communication channels opened by this committee were crucial to the success of future EdTech initiatives.

Change agents alone cannot influence their organization. It is crucial to create a team of individuals who are risk-takers, have open minds, and have the heart and passion to bring change to the organization (Change Agent Roles and Skills, 2013). I was fortunate to work with key people who shared a similar vision and who had the same passion and needed to see a change in the way technology was perceived and embraced in our institution. Professor Kate Lyons joined me early in this fascinating journey of adoption of innovation and culture change; with her degrees in librarianship and non-profit management, she brought different perspectives to the table. Dr. Kate Wolfe joined us in 2015, and Dr. Kristopher Burrell in 2016. Along with the partnership with Lyons, Wolfe, and Burrell, I was fortunate to have the support of the EdTech team, a group of exceptional instructional design specialists, whose commitment to the success of all the projects the office encompassed exceeded their responsibilities. The team has changed somewhat over the years, but has benefited from the stability of a few staff members that have been part of EdTech since the first days of the office, specifically George Rosa and Iber Poma, and later Wilfredo Rodriguez. Their experience, relationships with faculty, shared vision, and knowledge of the culture of the university have helped to guide the new members of the EdTech team during all these years.

The provost appointed me to co-direct the Hostos Center for Teaching and Learning (CTL) in 2015. It was an opportunity to reimagine the role of CTL and the way it was integrated with the Office of Educational Technology. It was also an opportunity to reinforce existing initiatives and promote new ones that resulted from pedagogical inquiry and focused on improving teaching practices that lead to higher levels of student participation and success, all with an implicit lens of technology as an enabler. As with the EdTech team, I have been fortunate to have an exceptional team at CTL who go above and beyond the call of duty. During my four years as co-director, I have had the opportunity to work with faculty co-directors, including my current co-director, Professor Cynthia Jones. Having the opportunity to lead CTL, EdTech, and several advisory councils (including the Educational Technology Leadership Council, the CTL Advisory Council, CUNY CTL Advisory Council, and research groups inside and outside of my university), as well as chair the Hostos Higher Education Officers Organization gave me the opportunity to have direct contact with faculty and learn from their experiences, understand their needs, celebrate their successes and, consequently, learn the insights of the culture of my organization.

In addition to co-directors, faculty, and an excellent team of educational technologists, I have been extremely fortunate to have the support and confidence of senior management on my journey of organizational culture change. Over the past ten years, Hostos' senior leadership has provided vision and energy to push the boundaries to achieve higher graduation rates, faculty scholarship, and innovation in all of our practices. Specifically in the area of technology, Hostos has excelled among the colleges of the City University of New York and beyond. These factors included the unfailing support of the current college president, Dr. David Gómez, and provost, Dr. Christine Mangino. I am also fortunate that Chief Information Officer (CIO) Varun Sehgal, the Information Technology team, and all members of senior management have allowed me and my team to take risks, be innovative, and continuously seek new ways to enhance teaching and learning. The overall success of this process, from my perspective, has two components—the ability to cultivate and embrace the strengths and diverse perspectives of team members while shifting their mindset from a team member to an agent of change; and the ability to cultivate relationships and partnerships with strategic stakeholders, and buy-in and support of senior management, while recognizing the efforts of faculty and staff who take risks and innovate.

As I intuited back in 2002 when I began my professional career at Hostos, innovation and constant change *are* my job, which means that I have to constantly look for new ways in which emerging technologies can improve teaching and learning and finding ways to communicate these benefits to faculty and administrators. I am in the business of continuous risk-taking, trial and error, and culture change. I have lived my career with the mindset that for every challenge there is an opportunity, and the beauty of my job is that I am uniquely positioned to identify opportunities for each new technology or approach to teaching, which is something that I love. Having an open mind, cultivating acceptance by senior management and key stakeholders, developing and fostering the team, and using the power of the network have been key in ensuring that our initiatives are supported and I am certain they have contributed to the advancement of the Hostos community as we deepen our culture of learning and innovation, and as we foster a network of confident and successful innovators.

Implementing and supporting change in the culture of an organization has no beginning and no end point, especially when it comes to technological innovation; successful change requires continuous nurturing and motivating to establish and maintain an active community of practice. In my years at Hostos, I have worked with colleagues to establish a solid framework of interconnected and interdependent artifacts, a framework that I call the Innovations Web. Successful change requires constant evaluation of initiatives and activities, professional development and support approaches, recognition practices, strategies for dissemination, and team knowledge and capacity building. I persistently work closely with my team to make these practices part of the DNA of the office and the way we do business. For each iteration, there is a great reward, which strengthens the Innovations Web and promotes innovation and culture change through an active community of practice. This framework encourages faculty to take risks in a safe, supportive environment and celebrate innovation, and the role of the EdTech team is to keep this framework constantly evolving. Chapter 3 will explain in more detail the Innovations Web and its components at Hostos.

References

Change Agent Roles and Skills. (2013). In M. H. Ferrara (Ed.), *Gale business insights handbook of cultural transformation* (pp. 47–56). Detroit, MI: Gale. Retrieved from http://link.galegroup.com.hostos.ezproxy.cuny.edu/apps/doc/CX2759200012/GVRL?u=cuny_bron60695&sid=GVRL&xid=4a52f7be

Elsayed, H., Guevara, C., Hoda-Kearse, R., Li, I., Lyons, K., Rosa, G., & Sehgal, V. (2013). Beyond physical space: Implementing a virtual learning commons at an urban community college. In R. G. Carpenter (Ed.), *Cases on higher education spaces: Innovation, collaboration, and technology* (pp. 207–229). Hershey, PA: IGI Global.

Pascale, R. T., & Sternin, J. (2005, May). Your company's secret change agents. *Harvard Business Review.* Retrieved from http://www.thelearningcoalition.org/wp-content/uploads/2012/10/Your%20Company's%20Secret%20Change%20Agents.pdf

CHAPTER 3

Change Management in Practice: Creating a Culture That Promotes Technology Adoption

Carlos Guevara, Kate Lyons, and Kate S. Wolfe

Change agents influence social processes within an organizational culture, and this culture is part of what affects technology adoption. In his book, *The Diffusion of Innovations*, developed by Rogers in 1962 tried to explain the potentially predictable spread of new ideas and new technologies (2003). The EdTech team at Hostos Community College developed a strategy to use Rogers' predictable framework for technology adoption, Kotter's writing on change management (2002), and Senge's (2006) five

---

C. Guevara (✉)
Division of Academic Affairs, Hostos Community College, CUNY, Bronx, NY, USA
e-mail: cguevara@hostos.cuny.edu

K. Lyons
Hostos Community College, CUNY, Bronx, NY, USA
e-mail: clyons@hostos.cuny.edu

K. S. Wolfe
Behavioral and Social Sciences Department, Hostos Community College, CUNY, Bronx, NY, USA
e-mail: kwolfe@hostos.cuny.edu

© The Author(s) 2019
K. S. Wolfe et al. (eds.), *Developing Educational Technology at an Urban Community College*, https://doi.org/10.1007/978-3-030-17038-7_3

principles for becoming a learning organization to guide their strategies for reaching the office's educational-technology adoption goals. The team also later added Schein's (2010) cultural-analysis levels to their plan. This chapter discusses the values the EdTech team decided to espouse, their efforts to develop their own cohesive relationships and their defining of an innovators group at Hostos, and the discussions about management theories they used as a tool for planning and reflection. This chapter also introduces the Innovations Web, a faculty and staff development framework created by Carlos Guevara for visualizing the desired culture change.

Identifying Risk-Taking, Community-Building, and Innovation as Core Values

As the EdTech team experienced a transition process in 2010, they realized that they needed more than just a set of goals and tasks. They also needed a set of shared values and an understanding that all team members should work toward the same goals and that similar values would be driving their decisions. Based on the lessons learned over the past ten years, the team's first step was to identify the values that would guide them and the organization. They agreed that encouraging faculty to be risk-takers, community-builders, and innovators would be crucial for an organizational culture that promotes the adoption of educational technology. Change provokes a series of reactions, both positive and negative, and requires faculty to move outside their comfort zones and take risks; therefore, establishing a safe environment for these traits to flourish was a goal for Guevara, the EdTech staff, and the liaisons. Carefully considering the reasons why the team selected its values helped create that safe environment. EdTech team members were always willing to discuss these core values and share why they were encouraged, and they were also open to questioning and reexamining these values.

Of the values that the EdTech team wanted to promote, innovation topped the list. For the team, being *innovative* meant that the faculty would try to implement new technologies and new teaching practices, often before best practices for those strategies were developed. Being innovative meant being the faculty and staff that did the job of developing those best practices. The team recognized that being identified as innovators within Rogers' innovation adoption curve (2003) would require a significant amount of trial and error, and accepting the faults and errors that inevitably occur. For a midsize public college like Hostos without resources to spare, the EdTech team had to consider the possibility of encouraging faculty to be in the innovators group of the innovation curve. In many ways, waiting until others have already developed the best practices and then doing research on new strategies to integrate teaching and technologies would be a more secure and pragmatic use of resources such as time and money.

The rationale of the EdTech team to prioritize innovation was ultimately based on two reasons. First, Hostos students tend to be nontraditional and could be better served by unconventional and more flexible ways to get them involved and engaged with education. Scaffolding and differentiated learning that are commonly seen in online courses, with the option for students to progress through the lessons at their own pace and convenience, made sense. Other educational technologies also offer students and faculty more flexibility and more ways to present content. Hostos' faculty seemed eager to try out new technologies to present their content in different ways and were especially eager to try out new technologies, such as lecture capture, so that students could review lectures repeatedly at their own pace. The EdTech team also believed that access to technology at the college would better prepare Hostos students for the workplace. Innovation with educational technology could improve educational outcomes for students. Secondly, faculty members who worked on projects with EdTech had greater scholarship opportunities. Historically, and during the period of change discussed in this book, the work of the faculty was generally well received at conferences, and many professors and staff members published scholarly articles about their work with the new educational technologies. Working together and collaborating also meant that these committed faculty members took time to reflect on their own teaching practices, which generally leads to better teaching practices (DuFour, 2004).

To a large extent, risk-taking goes hand in hand with innovation. For some faculty, the consequence of taking risks in the classroom could mean a waste of time or money. Faculty would devote their own time to developing new assignments, projects, and learning technology; they could also invest their own money in software or hardware licenses and not end up using their work in the classroom. Some faculty saw the risk for the students; being assigned to use a new technology meant that they would have to spend time learning the technology, which might not be the most efficient use of their time. In certain cases, the risks were greater. For example, in some departments, teachers needed to discuss the value of the new technology with their colleagues, and not all colleagues were so open to that discussion. In order to encourage faculty to take these risks, the EdTech team tried to mitigate the consequences of failure, as well as frame these risks as opportunities.

Finally, community building was crucial for EdTech to promote. The team needed the faculty that was already using educational technology to help them promote this among others on campus and to help guide those who are new to educational technology, especially in the case of online learning. The EdTech office in Hostos has a limited number of staff, which is not enough to offer personalized help to all interested parties; however, encouraging a group of champions to develop and nurture that community helped increase EdTech's reach. The EdTech team, in order to create community, organized events and also organized team building opportunities. The team recognized that if the adoption of the technology was to follow the path described by Rogers (2003), they had to focus on people rather than technology itself. It would be not only about offering access to something new and sending marketing blasts to the entire campus community, but about fostering on-campus communities that combine specific technologies in a natural way and then encouraging these communities to grow.

Team Development and Building a Community of Innovators

As described in Chap. 1, the EdTech Team is comprised of the director, staff, and faculty liaisons (initially Professor Kate Lyons, then Dr. Kate Wolfe, and finally Dr. Kristopher Burrell). In addition, there was a small but well-established group of faculty members who were interested in integrating technology into their teaching. These faculty members were already teaching online, and, in some cases, they were some of the few faculty who had tested online teaching as early as the 1990s, near the start of CUNY's online education forays. This group supported the EdTech team, spoke positively about technology, and expressed interest in being part of the majority of what EdTech offered. The EdTech team recognized the value of this group's support and created an internal mailing list of around 40 faculty, named EdTech Innovators, created professional development activities specifically for this group, and tried to find opportunities for them to come together to collaborate on projects. This group also became a source of people who the team could rely on when they started initiatives that needed mentors to help others who wanted to participate.

Although the study of diffusion theory predates Rogers, he popularized it in his book, *Diffusion of Innovations* (2003). Salter described Rogers' theory about the rate of adoption:

> The rate of adoption rises slowly at first. When around 20% of the population has joined, the adoption 'takes off.' The rate increases to a maximum when adoption reaches about 50% of the population. After this period of

rapid growth, the rate of adoption gradually stabilizes and may even decline. (p. 923)

The idea of a point when adoption "takes off" seemed crucial to EdTech at Hostos Community College, as did the idea of adopter categories. Salter (2005) described how, in Roger's theory:

> Individuals can be placed into adopter categories based on specific characteristics in relation to a proposed innovation. These categories are innovators, early adopters, early majority, late majority, and laggards. The *s*-shaped curve relates to the timing of adoption by the various categories. (p. 923)

Moore (1995) agreed and went further in emphasizing that the most difficult step in innovation adoption is transitioning from the early adopters (visionaries) to the early majority (pragmatists), and identified it as "crossing the chasm" (p. 17). Moore also stated that when an organization builds and maintains the momentum of the innovation through the "chasm," the organization will experience a culture shift (p. 9).

The EdTech team's approach was to encourage and nurture the groups on the left side of the curve—the innovators and early adopters. With their support, the approach was to reach out to other faculty members, and generally to visibly model technology adoption, thereby promoting EdTech initiatives to eventually arrive at that critical point where they "take off" (Salter, 2005) and reach the majority of faculty members. Through initiatives that strongly foster collaboration and the development of mentoring relationships between faculty members, the EdTech team's goal was that the innovators would approach the early adopters first, then the early majority, and eventually take off, until the majority of faculty members were integrating some technology into their teaching. Certainly, different disciplines and departments fit better with certain types of technology, but the goal was that all sections of all courses would at least have a Blackboard component, and that all faculty would be aware of and interested in exploring appropriate technology for their disciplines.

In fact, this did happen to an extent, and by 2016 more than 50% of course sections at Hostos had activated Blackboard sites and added some content to their course shells. Many additional courses integrated other online technology besides or in addition to Blackboard, like ePortfolios, iPads and associated apps; faculty members were also experimenting with lecture capture, other video/content creation tools, and recently virtual reality. Although the percentage of faculty taking advantage of technology in their teaching is not yet at 100%, it has increased quite a bit—to almost 80% as of 2018—according to the director of Educational Technology.

Hatton (2002) described the connection between the diffusion of innovations theory and change management, saying, "Diffusion of innovations is a theory originally designed to explain how change agents influence social processes" (p. 982). Additionally, Hatton explained how the theory has been applied more recently. "It has become a theory used to address how a technology or technological artifact becomes adopted, what forces affect the adoption process, and how proponents of a given technology or artifact may better influence the adoption process. The theory addressed how new ideas and technologies are communicated, evaluated, adopted, and reevaluated" (Hatton, 2002, p. 982). The EdTech team saw the theory as a way to propagate the message and as a part of a framework for understanding how the message could ripple through the organization.

In previous years, EdTech tried a variety of ways to encourage faculty to integrate technology into teaching—usually workshops, either one-day or multi-day, online or in-person, sometimes incentivized and sometimes not—and they had success in delivering content that way. Through those early attempts, what the EdTech team now refers to as EdTech Innovators was formed. This early foundation of the EdTech Innovators was key for moving to the next step in technology adoption, which was the plan to build communities around technology initiatives and encourage peers to teach each other. Several chapters discuss in more depth the Hybrid and Asynchronous Online Teaching Initiatives and the initiatives structured around specific technologies, such as lecture-capture software, using ePortfolios, and exploring apps for iPads used in the classroom. As the EdTech team increasingly saw the value of leveraging communities of practice to encourage technology adoption, they decided to purposefully nurture this group of innovators and provide opportunities for active participation in this community of innovators.

Bonding While Discussing Management Theory: An Approach to Team Building

Higgins and McAllaster (2004), based on their research about organizational culture, described it "as the pattern of shared values and norms that distinguishes one organization from another. These shared values and norms indicate what is believed to be important in the organization – what is of value to organizational members" (p. 66). For the EdTech team, it was fundamental to analyze the culture of Hostos, in particular the aspect of the culture driving faculty's likelihood to adopt new technology in their teaching. They then planned to establish intentional initiatives that would lead to the sustained acceptance of organizational values that would drive the needed charges for technology adoption. Schein (2010) proposed three levels of cultural analysis to take into account when learning about the essence of the culture or its DNA: (a) artifacts and behaviors; (b) espoused beliefs and values; (c) basic underlying assumptions (p. 17). He describes artifacts as behaviors and set processes, espoused beliefs and values as the organization and staff members' missions and goals, and underlying assumptions as unconscious beliefs and values (Schein, 2010, pp. 17–30).

Being cognizant of the theory of learning organizations and its principles, which Senge prescribed for an organization to cultivate a culture of learning, was important to the EdTech team. Senge (2006) illustrated five principles needed for an organizational culture that is nimble and adaptable. He noted that workers have personal and professional development goals and a desire for "personal mastery" of their tasks and skills. Also, workers have a shared vision, meaning that the goals of individuals align with that of the organization, which has a culture that makes the effort to understand the framework for effective organizations. Senge states that team learning has to be prioritized and individuals should strive for shared decision-making and mutual accountability. Finally, he notes the importance of systems alignment, the principle that binds the other four and requires a holistic view of the organization. The EdTech team understood the importance of seeing the organization as a living organism and the impact any intervention can have on the organization. To visualize how the different elements connect and support to nurture this learning organization and promote culture change, Guevara illustrated the Innovators Web framework.

The Innovations Web

Based on the theories described in the previous section, the EdTech team realized that there was a need to establish a framework to help visualize the interconnected and interdependent nature of all initiatives, the artifacts created, and the service-and-support approach. This framework would foster the type of systems thinking described by Senge, and change management necessary to apply the diffusion of innovation theory described by Hatton. The idea behind the Innovations Web is that all initiatives and artifacts are interconnected nodes (or pillars), each with a role that can have a positive or negative impact on the overall strength of this connected web. Guevara describes six main nodes that play a more important role in the nurturing and strengthening of the other nodes in the Innovations Web: (a) Ideas Generator, (b) Support Structure, (c) Dissemination and Outreach, (d) Community Building, (e) Continuous Improvement, (f) Innovators Recognition (Fig. 3.1).

The *Ideas Generator* node provides a visualization of a safe space to explore new ideas, technologies, and teaching approaches. This is the node where the brainstorming and initial planning occurs, where the seed of an idea begins; through the other nodes, it can mature into pilot initiatives and possibly be accepted as an institutionalized practice. Examples of results from the Ideas Generator node, which will be described in detail in the next chapters, include initiatives such as iPads in the classroom, a proj-

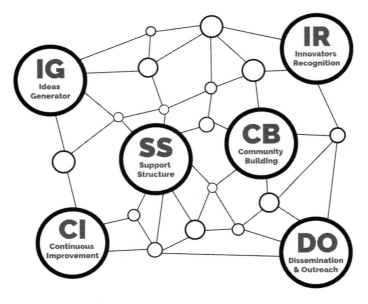

Fig. 3.1 Innovations Web

ect for the development of lecture capture, the creation of a committee on the adoption of ePortfolios, and other initiatives on active learning and virtual/augmented reality. The generation of ideas occurs everywhere and at any time, but, if there are no spaces created to intentionally capture these ideas, opportunities for innovation could be lost.

At Hostos, the establishment of spaces such as advisory councils, task forces, faculty inquiry groups, teaching days, common-reading initiatives, professional development retreats, celebration and recognition of innovations, and more provide a safe space for the exploration and capture of new ideas that can lead to the flourishing of initiatives or the adoption of best practices. The strength of this node lies in identifying all the different ways of creating spaces to share ideas and exchange experiences and perspectives on the use of technology. Determining which of these forms would work depends to a large extent on the culture of the organization, and, like the way in which the adoption of innovation is initially conceived, there will be many trials and errors until the structures, activities, and places are seen as safe spaces to share.

The *Support Structure* node ensures that innovators feel safe and supported in the exploration of new ideas and technologies. The EdTech team became aware of the need to prioritize a support system for faculty who use technology for the first time in their teaching through the evaluation of the successes and failures of previous initiatives, and by listening to the experiences of the faculty who shared the obstacles in their ways to integrate new technologies or change their pedagogical approaches. There was also a clear need for better support for students to take advantage of new technologies, especially for students in online courses. Instructional designers, faculty mentors, design interns, and technology assistants are part of the support structure that helps create this safe environment. The EdTech Office implemented an open-door policy where faculty or students do not need to schedule an appointment to receive support from any member of the EdTech team.

The EdTech team noted that the path to finding support should be more transparent for students and advocated for changing and combining administrative processes to increase transparency. For example, in some cases, the organization of services reflected the hierarchical divisions of the offices, which are good for administrative purposes but not necessarily for the end user. A student or instructor does not need to know that Unit X is providing a particular service and that, if they need something more related, Unit Y must provide them, which confuses and forces students to understand the internal structures of these units. From the point of view of the user, if they require a service or support for a particular need, they do not need to know the internal processes of these services; they only need a solution for their need. It was a priority of the EdTech team to work together with other units and departments on campus to ensure that end users would receive appropriate and quick referrals to the right areas and that they would be served as best as they could by any administrator or staff member they found. At Hostos, there are many examples of the creation of these synergies and, particularly from the technological and pedagogical areas, there has been an evolution in this area (see Section II).

The *Dissemination and Outreach* node focuses on establishing clear structures to communicate resources, support, initiatives, and opportunities to innovate teaching practices through technology. The message must be coherent, concise, and attractive to the target audience. The media must be varied enough to reflect the different channels used by the college community, from printing, email, the web, text messages, social networks, to word of mouth. EdTech established a brand strategy to promote the initiatives and keep the college community informed and excited about innovation opportunities. The EdTech team changed its name from Instructional Technology to Educational Technology (EdTech) as an initial effort to establish an effective communication structure. Several communication devices were created to further improve their brand change and outreach efforts, such as the Innovation newsletter, email blasts called "Tips of the Week" and "Tips of the Month", professional development calendars (available in both print and digital form), social media pages, website updates, a video channel, text messages, and more. Another important element of this node is the dissemination of the results of the work and the achievements of the initiatives created by the EdTech team through various channels, such as conference presentations, research studies, and publications.

The *Community Building* node focuses on establishing ways to effectively keep the members of the organization engaged. Along with the support for the generation of ideas, the establishment of spaces for the faculty to meet together serves as a driver for building the community and disseminating the initiatives, support services and activities offered by EdTech. On campus, EdTech realized that email opening rates were minimal and seemed to have decreased over the years, and that the most effective dissemination tool would be word of mouth. All committee meetings and faculty inquiry groups, professional development activities, and innovation celebrations have been the perfect tools to convey the message and keep the teaching community informed and engaged.

The *Continuous Improvement* node focuses on ensuring the continuous evaluation of the different initiatives and technological innovations at Hostos. Professional development and new-technology pilot programs were planned together with evaluative instruments to determine the qualitative and quantitative impact and relevance of such technologies for teaching and learning. The EdTech team works closely with the Office of Institutional Research to analyze the different performance indicators of the courses that piloted a specific technology. The results of the analysis and satisfaction surveys provide opportunities for the improvement and continuous development of approaches and initiatives. To continue studying the development and implementation of online learning and new initiatives at Hostos, the creation of the Hostos Online Learning Assessment task force (HOLA) has been fundamental. The results of research conducted on the perceptions of students and faculty about online learning have led to the establishment and/or improvement of initiatives and professional development (see Chap. 16).

The *Innovators Recognition* node focuses on strengthening and cultivating excellence through recognizing the risk-takers, pioneers, mentors, early adopters, and community-builders with a vision centered around promoting innovation, risk-taking, and community-building. It was very important for the EdTech team to acknowledge the amount of work innovators invest in trying new things above their already saturated workload comprised of teaching, research, service, and so on. As a result, EdTech established a structure to show appreciation and recognition of their contributions to teaching and learning. A number of artifacts were created to establish this structure; for example, the Innovation Celebration is an event celebrated every semester to recognize the top innovators and to create a space to nurture the community of innovators at Hostos. During this celebration, new technologies are introduced, and great networking, food, prizes, and a celebratory cake are part of these celebrations. The Innovation Chase is another artifact that was introduced in 2014, which consists of a system of digital badges that represent use of and expertise in different technology or new pedagogical strategies adopted by faculty. It uses a game-based learning approach to encourage continuous participation and healthy competition, as each badge that faculty earn has points that accumulate and are used to identify the top innovators who are recognized at the Innovation Celebrations (see Chap. 9).

Another artifact that was created to strengthen this node and others is a conference that extends beyond Hostos Community College, which provides an opportunity to showcase the innovative work faculty have been doing in the classroom. This conference was born in 2013 and is the result of a collaboration among the three Bronx CUNY colleges: Bronx Community College, Hostos Community College, and Lehman College. The goals of this initiative are to bring together faculty from community colleges and senior colleges, provide a venue to share best practices and experiences in trying out new ideas or technologies, and, most importantly, to promote cross-institutional and cross-disciplinary collaborations (see Chap. 6).

Niemiec (2017), in an article in *Psychology Today*, compiled some different definitions of mindfulness. He stated: "Mindfulness means paying attention on purpose, in the present moment and without prejudice" and "Mindfulness is the self-regulation of attention with an attitude of curiosity, openness and acceptance." The EdTech team intentionally tried to create a community of innovators in Hostos. The team devoted considerable effort to reflect on the behavior of the organization and how to create change in a way that supports and encourages faculty and staff on campus. While the values that the EdTech team wanted to encourage were risk-taking, community-building, and innovation, the team also tried to lead with a focus that was supportive, egalitarian, and self-aware. The members of the team tried to reflect in a conscious way on their behaviors and attitudes, and to lead with openness.

References

DuFour, R. (2004). Schools as learning communities. *Educational Leadership, 61*(8), 6–86. Retrieved from http://search.ebscohost.com/login.aspx?direct=true&db=eue&AN=507907990&site=ehost-live

Hatton, M. L. (2002). Technology, adoption and diffusion of. In J. R. Schement (Ed.), *Encyclopedia of communication and information* (Vol. 3, pp. 982–985). New York: Macmillan Reference. Retrieved from http://link.galegroup.com/apps/doc/CX3402900269/GVRL?u=cuny_bron60695&sid=GVRL&xid=c3196261

Higgins, J. M., & McAllaster, C. (2004). If you want strategic change, don't forget to change your cultural artifacts. *Journal of Change Management, 4*(1), 63–73. https://doi.org/10.1080/1469701032000154926.

Kotter, J. P. (2002). *The heart of change*. Boston: Harvard Business School Publishing.

Moore, G. A. (1995). *Crossing the chasm: Marketing and selling high-tech products to mainstream customers.* New York: Harper Business.

Niemiec, R. M. (2017, November 1). 3 definitions of mindfulness that might surprise you. *Psychology Today.* Retrieved from https://www.psychologytoday.com/us/blog/what-matters-most/201711/3-definitions-mindfulness-might-surprise-you

Rogers, E. M. (2003). *Diffusion of innovations* (5th ed.). New York: Simon and Schuster.

Salter, G. (2005). Factors affecting the adoption of educational technology. In C. Howard, J. V. Boettcher, & L. Justice (Eds.), *Encyclopedia of distance learning* (Vol. 2, pp. 922–929). Hershey, PA: Idea Group Reference. Retrieved from http://link.galegroup.com/apps/doc/CX3466600158/GVRL?u=cuny_bron60695&sid=GVRL&xid=e3795673

Schein, E. H. (2010). *Organizational culture and leadership.* San Francisco: Jossey-Bass.

Senge, P. M. (2006). *The fifth discipline: The art and practice of the learning organization.* New York: Currency and Doubleday.

CHAPTER 4

Who We Are and Why It Matters

Elys Vasquez-Iscan

Eugenio María de Hostos Community College was the eighth proposed community college within The City University of New York. As stated in its original proposal by the Board of Higher Education, Hostos "will fulfill the functions of a comprehensive community college, serve the needs of a poverty area, and provide extensive and unique opportunities in education for health cares" (April, 1968). As a comprehensive community college, it was designed to provide college education as well as adult-and-continuing-education programs. Hostos Community College was created to be innovative in providing a broad range of health and social-service academic programs that would meet the growing demand for skilled health-care workers in New York City. Since its inception in 1968, Hostos has attended to the diverse needs of New York City's underserved population by offering full-time, part-time, and evening college degree programs as well as the provision of non-degree or certificate programs. Currently, Hostos provides an expansive array of online and hybrid courses to support students' academic persistence and degree completion. Although Hostos has since celebrated its 50th anniversary, its mission continues to be one of social justice. The college educates and promotes social mobility among diverse student populations that

E. Vasquez-Iscan (✉)
Hostos Community College, CUNY, Bronx, NY, USA
e-mail: evasquez-iscan@hostos.cuny.edu

© The Author(s) 2019
K. S. Wolfe et al. (eds.), *Developing Educational Technology at an Urban Community College*, https://doi.org/10.1007/978-3-030-17038-7_4

have been historically marginalized. These populations include students from low-income neighborhoods, communities of color, immigrants, and the justice-involved.

Hostos Community College Student and Faculty Demographics

The Hostos Community College student demographic is mostly composed of Hispanics (57%), African Americans (21%), and females (67%) (Hostos Community College Office of Institutional Research and Student Assesment, 2018). The average age of a Hostos student is 25 years (HCC OIRSA, 2018). The student demographic at Hostos follows the national enrollment profile of community-college students. The National Center for Education Statistics (2018) reports that, in fall 2017, 44% of Hispanic undergraduate students and 35% of Black undergraduate students were enrolled at a community college (HCC OIRSA, 2018). Hostos, as a community college in the South Bronx, is a gateway to postsecondary education for students of low socioeconomic status who are often first-generation college attendees. National data reports that 44% of low-income students (those with family incomes of less than $25,000 per year) attend community colleges after high school, compared with 15% of high-income students (National Center for Public Policy and Higher Education, 2011). Comparably, 38% of students whose parents did not graduate from college report a community college as their first postsecondary enrollment institution, compared with 20% of students whose parents graduated from college (National Center for Public Policy and Higher Education, 2011).

The Hostos full-time faculty demographic composition is White (43% female and 45% male), Hispanic (26% female and 25% male), and Black (18% female and 9% male) (CUNY Office of Institutional Research and Assesment, 2018). The majority (42.9%) of the full-time faculty are between 50 and 64 years of age followed by the age group 35–49 years (30.2%) (CUNY OIRA, 2018). Moreover, most of the full-time faculty (86%) have tenure (CUNY OIRA, 2018).

Hostos, as a community anchor, provides more than just academic programs. The college offers cultural events and countless community-collaborative programs. Hostos' ongoing legacy of providing education as a tool for social mobility to diverse student populations has enabled students who reported being in the bottom 20% of household income to achieving incomes in the top 20% upon degree completion (Aisch, Buchanan, Cox, & Quealy, 2017). These student outcomes have garnered

Hostos attention across the country. Hostos is part of the City University of New York (CUNY), which is the largest public and urban university system in the country. Moreover, within CUNY community colleges, Hostos reported having the highest "intergenerational social mobility rate" of students (Aisch et al., 2017). Therefore, Hostos, as an academic institution educating underserved populations, is in a strategic position to promote educational technology among its student population.

Hostos has become a national innovator among community colleges using educational technology to improve student learning, engagement, and services. Such efforts have been recognized by the Center for Digital Education (CDE), which ranked Hostos as the top Digital Community College in 2016. In the most recent national survey conducted by the CDE, "Hostos placed second overall in the nation among mid-sized colleges" (Grenslitt, 2018). Noteworthy to mention is Hostos' continuous top-ten ranking—eight times—as a digital community college. Hostos continually strives to use educational technology to foster an engaging learning atmosphere inside and outside the classroom that supports students' academic persistence and degree completion. Furthermore, Hostos utilizes educational technology to support faculty in adopting innovative teaching modalities that promote active learning and enhance their pedagogy.

FACTORS CONTRIBUTING TO ONLINE LEARNING AT COMMUNITY COLLEGES

There has been a growing national trend in the enrollment of online courses at public two-year colleges (Jaggars, 2014). The open-admissions policy of community colleges attracts a diverse student population that is non-traditional in demographic makeup (Jaggars, 2014). Community-college students tend to be older than the four-year college students, are enrolled part-time, and employed full-time (Jaggars, 2014). Online courses offer community-college students a flexible and convenient schedule that allows them to fulfill multiple responsibilities (i.e. work and family).

In a survey conducted at Hostos Community College, approximately one-fourth of the student respondents reported taking online courses due to their flexibility and convenience, which allows them to fulfill their work or family commitments (Wolfe, DiSanto, Poma, & Rodriguez, 2018). Another factor influencing student enrollment in online courses is their perceived ease of learning the subject. According to Jaggars, most students prefer online courses in subject areas they identify as easy and prefer to take face-to-face courses in subjects they consider to be difficult such as Math and Science (2014). A third factor influencing student enrollment in online courses is the student's regard for the subject. Jaggars noted that students were averse to taking online courses in subjects they held in high regard such as courses in their major (2014). Students who struggle with certain subjects prefer the face-to-face classroom environment where they feel supported. Jaggars noted that a consistent level of interactive technology that facilitates student-instructor relationships is needed (2014).

Recent data shows community colleges as having a pivotal role in shaping the academic and career trajectory of most students with a bachelor's degree. According to a report from the National Student Clearinghouse Research Center, of those students who received a four-year college degree in academic year 2015–2016, 49% had been enrolled at a two-year public institution in the previous ten years (2017). The National Center for Public Policy and Higher Education estimates that 40% of all enrollments in higher education are from community colleges (2011). As a community college, Hostos' student population mirrors the national student trend at community colleges, which experiences high rates of poverty coupled with the need to take various remedial courses for several semesters before being able to take college-level courses. According to a study conducted by the Community College Research Center, among 250,000 students at 57 community colleges, it was reported that 59% of new students were referred to Developmental Math and 33% were referred to Developmental Reading (Bailey, Jeong, & Cho, 2010). Data from a national study showed that 58% of recent high school graduates who enrolled in community colleges had to take at least one developmental course (Attewell, Lavin, Domnia, & Levey, 2006). Completion of remedial courses is usually correlated with a student's ability to stay in college and receive a bachelor's degree. Remediation assists students who are poorly prepared for college academic work by providing basic skills and/or knowledge. At Hostos, 37.1% of first-year students are in a remedial Math course and 8.5% are in an English remedial course (HCC OIRSA, 2018).

As first-year students progress in their academic trajectory at Hostos, they enroll in online courses. Two studies analyzing the performance of community-college students in online courses demonstrated the students' decrease in academic performance in fully online courses (CCRC, 2013; Xu & Jaggars, 2014). However, it is noted that such poor academic performance in online courses was mainly noted among lower performing students who also experienced poor academic performance in face-to-face courses. In online courses, students who already demonstrate poor academic performance in face-to-face courses are more likely to drop out of the online class or experience a more pronounced performance gap. Xu and Jaggars observed that, for students with a grade point average (GPA) less than 3.02, they are 2% more likely to drop out of an in-person course than a student with a GPA greater than 3.02 (2014). By comparison, in online courses, students with poor academic performance are 4% more likely to drop out of the course. With challenges of student remediation and low socioeconomic status that perpetuate a digital divide among students, Hostos aims to provide universal access to educational technology that may mitigate the various obstacles that community-college students currently face. In contrast to national data that shows a decrease in the academic performance of community-college students in online courses (CCRC, 2013; Xu & Jaggars, 2014), Hostos students tend to show similar academic performance in online and face-to-face courses. By Hostos allowing remedial students to simultaneously take college-credit courses, these students receive ample preparation for the demands of online courses. Moreover, through the utilization of various theoretical frameworks (i.e. pedagogy of the oppressed and communal constructivism), Hostos uses educational technology as a social equalizer that prompts students to become better prepared for the technology-driven workforce.

Using Constructs from Pedagogy of the Oppressed to Promote Educational Technology

Hostos was founded on the heels of the American civil rights movement and the women's liberation movement, which led Hostos to be focused on social activism. This prompts students to become social-change agents. One of the focus areas of pedagogy of the oppressed is to identify systems of oppression that perpetuate the subjugation of the people (Freire, 1970, 2018). As Hostos strives to integrate technology into more of its courses, students have the potential to lose the fear of technology and discover an appreciation for newly acquired skills or skills that they were not aware they possessed. However, without adequate access to technology off campus, this growth in technological skills may be stymied.

Technology offers a myriad of possibilities, although these benefits are not equally distributed in society (see Chap. 5). This creates a digital divide that exacerbates the problems of oppression and exploitation as information is only being created and accessed by a limited number of people in society who are usually in positions of power and prestige. By integrating educational technology in courses, students become prepared for the workforce, but, most importantly, they will co-create society's norms for technology. As such, Hostos students who represent a historically marginalized and underserved population will embark on careers where they are underrepresented and create a paradigm shift leading to social change. The fields of technology and health care are highly underrepresented by minorities. Hostos academic-degree programs aim to increase the representation of minorities who are highly skilled professionals in these fields. Following Freire's pedagogy of the oppressed, professors and students are prompted to see each other as co-facilitators of learning where the instructor encourages students to see their personal plight as a source of knowledge rather than as a deficiency. This viewpoint enables students to increase their self-confidence and self-efficacy, thereby prompting them to embrace academic challenges. By students seeing instructors as a learning partner, a system of mentoring and support is created for students who often lack the knowledge of how to build social capital. It is through these achievements that students and instructors begin to make groundbreaking discoveries in and outside the classroom. Students gain an appreciation for learning and self-discovery, and faculty connect thoughts with concrete actions, achieving praxis.

Communal Constructivism for Online Learning

As Hostos continues to carry out its legacy of providing education for the historically marginalized, it also aims to empower this population. By utilizing the process of communal constructivism where learning is seen as a social and collaborative effort that is enabled rather than directly taught by the teacher, students are actively engaged in the learning process (Holmes, Tangney, Fitzgibbon, Savage, & Meehan, 2001). Communal constructivism is derived from the learning theory of constructivism that asserts that knowledge is not only created by learners via a formative process that depends on what is transmitted by the medium (i.e. instructor, text), but also in the way that the learner processes the content within the context of their current knowledge and experiences (Driscoll, 2000). Communal constructivism fosters the idea that students can construct their own knowledge as an outcome of interacting with their environment and become co-creators of knowledge for their learning community (Holmes et al., 2001).

Learning in the information age requires interaction with computers, which allows students to interface with various sources of information. Health science students in particular must learn to discern credible information from quackery. Utilizing a communal constructivist approach allows courses to be dynamic and adaptive to the students' need. Since peer support and group learning are promoted in this approach, students are provided with continual learning support from the instructor and their peers. Students also see themselves as co-creators of knowledge rather than just consumers of information (Holmes et al., 2001). The students at Hostos represent marginalized groups that society has ignored and rendered as unimportant, but, through communal constructivism, they become important learners who merit being heard. Moreover, their work and contributions in the classroom are acknowledged.

Diffusion of Online Learning as an Innovation of Educational Technology

What history has taught us about innovation is that all in the population rarely adopt it at a fast pace or at the same pace. The diffusion of innovation model is utilized to better understand the necessary steps and processes to attain broader dissemination and diffusion of innovations. Diffusion and dissemination are two distinct ideas. According to Rogers, diffusion is the process by which an innovation is conveyed through certain outlets over time among members of a social system (2003). Dissemination is a deliberate and systematic effort to enable the wide distribution and availability of an innovation (i.e. online courses) to an intended audience or members of a social system (Oldenburg & Glanz, 2008). In analyzing the diffusion and dissemination of online courses, it is important to understand faculty and student perceptions of such courses. Studies analyzing faculty perceptions of online courses report that computer self-efficacy, which is an individual's belief about personal abilities in using computers, and the perceived ease of use of educational technology impact faculty interest and satisfaction with teaching online (Wingo, Ivankova, & Moss, 2017). By comparison, studies analyzing student perceptions of online courses demonstrate that reasons why students enroll in online courses are flexibility, convenience, and perceived ease of learning the subject (Jaggars, 2014; Wolfe, et al., 2018). Noteworthy to mention is that the majority of student respondents in a survey at Hostos Community College reported online courses to be equally challenging as face-to-face courses (Wolfe et al., 2018). This finding challenges data from other studies that report students' perceptions of online courses as easier than face-to-face (Jaggars, 2014; Kauffman, 2015). However, it is important to acknowledge that the Hostos student population is heavily composed of students with remedial needs, and this may influence their perception of online courses (HCC OIRSA, 2018). The results of this study are shared in Chap. 16.

Faculty Perceptions of Teaching Online

Allen and Seaman observed that there is an increased demand for faculty to teach online courses in the United States (2015). A key success of online courses is their ability to provide millions of students with access to higher education, which they might be otherwise denied because of time or geographic challenges (Allen & Seaman, 2015). However, it is noted that one of the persistent failures of online education has been its inability to win the full support of faculty (Allen & Seaman, 2015). Over the past decade, faculty have shown a meager level of acceptance for online education as a valuable and legitimate mode of instruction (Allen & Seaman, 2015). According to Allen and Seaman, only 28% of chief academic officers reported that their faculty accepted the value and legitimacy of online education (2015). Based on the model of diffusion of innovation, faculty are more likely to accept online teaching if it is widespread at an institution.

At Hostos, the Office of Educational Technology (EdTech) offers faculty the opportunity for professional development by participating in the online-course development initiative. This initiative is held in high regard by the Hostos college administrators, and viewed by the college committees granting faculty tenure and promotion as part of faculty improving their pedagogy and professional development. Studies have shown that more faculty are motivated to teach online when they see the accomplishment of teaching online recognized and awarded by their academic institution (Bacow et al., 2012; Gautreau, 2011). Furthermore, student and faculty surveys at Hostos reinforce the importance that online courses have in supporting the strategic plan of the college. The Hostos

Community College Strategic Plan Framework for 2017–2022 focuses on increasing students' academic persistence and reducing the time to degree completion (HCC, 2017). Due to their flexible schedule and accessibility, online courses at Hostos can potentially enable students to complete their degree in a shorter time. As such, online teaching is becoming an integral component of the college's instructional culture. These factors have allowed Hostos faculty to appreciate the value and legitimacy of online teaching. Academic leadership at Hostos has also recognized the time-consuming effort that it takes for faculty to teach an online course as opposed to a face-to-face course. This recognition has translated into EdTech offering ongoing mentoring, instructional design and technical support through workshops, one-on-one trainings, and continuously enhancing the technologies used for teaching to improve the online-teaching experience for faculty. Furthermore, due to the heavier teaching load at community colleges as opposed to four-year colleges, online teaching offers community-college faculty more flexibility in their teaching schedule, which permits them to pursue additional scholarly endeavors such as research and publishing.

Whereas the majority of students express interest in online courses due to their flexible schedule and accessibility, faculty express interest in teaching online courses due to their flexible schedule, perceived usefulness (meaning the level to which one believes a technology will enhance his or her job performance), and perceived ease of use, which is the amount of effort an individual deems he or she will need to spend to master that technology (Wingo, Ivankova, & Moss, 2017). In addition to appreciating the flexible schedule that online teaching offers, faculty have also acknowledged the personal and professional development opportunities that online teaching offers (Allen & Seaman, 2015; McQuiggan, 2012) (see Chap. 7).

CHALLENGES AND STRENGTHS IN ADOPTING EDUCATIONAL TECHNOLOGY AMONG FACULTY

There is a substantial amount of research focusing on quality in college-level teaching. Such research asserts that students deem teachers to be effective when they are responsive, passionate, student-centered, professional, and content experts (Onwuegbuzie et al., 2007). Kester, Kirschner, and Corbalan noted that interaction is a key element in the learning environment (2006). Chen and Shaw also noted that, for students to have mastery over new and intricate course content, the information must be thoughtfully presented and instructor feedback should be prompt (2006). Chickering and Gamson have provided more than 50 years of research on college pedagogy and established seven dimensions of practice that are considered key elements of quality college instruction (1987). These seven dimensions entail faculty who encourage active learning, student-faculty interactions, collaborations among students, and prompt feedback to students, and who emphasize time on task, convey high expectations, and embrace diverse learning styles and talents (1987). The aforementioned dimensions are impacted by the skills of the instructor as well as the modality through which the instruction is delivered. Opponents of online teaching raise questions about the quality of student and instructor interactions, course design, and the ability of online courses to address the dimensions of instructional effectiveness offered by Chickering and Gamson. Omrod posited that students who are learning new and complex materials usually are not organized in their cognitive process and, therefore, are unable to prioritize and focus on the most important information in order to gain mastery (2004). Oh and Jonassen concluded that self-regulation of learning is difficult for most students and that students learning in online courses have challenges with understanding and applying information (2007).

Providing information to students or ensuring that students have access to information resources is not enough for the learning process. Such strategies do not align with the fundamental complexity of learning that requires mastery of rigorous course content through content application. Currently, there is limited research discussing the capacities of online instruction in attending to the dimensions of effective college learning and the systems utilized to teach online. Proponents for online teaching laud the innumerable potential that online media offers in the learning process.

It is noted that online media offers endless potential in enhancing interaction and student engagement. If they are deliberately designed, threaded discussions, e-mails, short video clips, and two-way audio offer a myriad of opportunities to enrich the learning environment for students. At Hostos, faculty are partaking in an initiative to utilize Panopto, a lecture-capture software that allows faculty to record their lectures as well as other teaching content that students can access via the college-learning management system (Blackboard). As part of expanding the diffusion of Panopto on campus, Ed Tech has fully integrated Panopto into Blackboard to allow easy access for any faculty interested in using Panopto. In addition to faculty creating content in Panopto, students are granted access by the course instructor to upload recordings of presentation projects, which are shared with the entire class via Blackboard. In this manner students contribute to course content and are actively engaged in their learning as they exchange information with their peers and the instructor (see Chap. 6).

As educators who are committed to online learning strive to provide a fully interactive learning environment that attends to the same multiple dimensions of teaching and learning often taking place in face-to-face interactions, they will continually have to explore interactive modalities that intrinsically motivate students and provide opportunities for students to apply newly gained information. EdTech offers faculty and student support in the form of training to utilize educational technology software such as Blackboard, Panopto, ePortfolios, iPads in the classroom, Virtual Reality, the Math Web App, among others, as well as tech support for faculty and students involved in asynchronous and hybrid courses. EdTech has supported several Mathematics instructors with the use of the Math Web App, who after several years of continuous use have reported high student satisfaction and, often, higher performance indicators compared with the sections of the course that do not use the app. Initial internal performance analysis was performed and showed results similar to those reported by the instructors who used the app. In addition, the Math Web App, as an educational technology tool, offers students the opportunity to apply learned content, which is one of the proposed dimensions of educational effectiveness offered by Chickering and Gamson (1987). The EdTech team plans to formalize these studies and publish the results to demonstrate the potential that the use of educational technology can have to improve Mathematics outcomes among remedial students at a minority-serving community college, specifically to increase the passing rate and reduce the number of students receiving an incomplete for the course.

In 2014, EdTech developed an award-winning online-readiness course, Are You Ready? This online course offers students the opportunity to assess their readiness to enroll in online courses and to learn the fundamental skills required to be an online learner. Enrollment in this online-readiness course is voluntary yet strongly recommended by faculty, particularly by faculty who teach asynchronous and hybrid courses (see Chap. 6).

Through a consortium of experts on campus composed of faculty and staff who are innovators and experienced online-course developers, EdTech provides faculty with training and mentoring in the development of asynchronous and hybrid courses. This ensures the integrity and uniformity of the design of online courses. The guidelines set for the design of online courses is based on national standards, and faculty receive training and mentoring over the period of one full semester before becoming certified to teach an online course. Once the course is delineated in the learning management system (Blackboard), a panel of faculty experts who have a substantial amount of experience teaching and designing online courses evaluate the newly designed online course and provide constructive and meaningful feedback to the course creator. Such feedback adheres to the established principles of online-course design set in the Online Learning Consortium Quality Scorecard, the California State University Chico Rubrics for Online Instruction, and the Quality Matters Rubric Standards. Moreover, throughout the mentoring and training process of online-course design it is emphasized to faculty that online courses are expected to be equivalent to a regular face-to-face course and should cover all the learning goals and objectives that a regular course does in a semester based on the college curriculum.

The Hostos online-course development guidelines highlight that what distinguishes an online course from a face-to-face course is the "mode of delivery not the content of the class" (HCC Ed Tech, 2019). Additionally, the EdTech office operates under an open-door policy for faculty and students, which should be beneficial for online students and faculty teaching online courses. This open-door policy ensures that faculty and students receive continued support throughout the teaching and learning process of an online course. It is noted that, when institutions provide continued mentoring, training, support, and recognition for teaching online, faculty are more receptive of online teaching. When the stakeholders at academic institutions consider faculty and student perceptions of online education, informed decisions about faculty training, student support, and educational technology selection can be achieved. Other important factors that institutions must consider to strengthen their online-teaching programs are integrating online teaching as part of the college strategic plan and faculty involvement in the planning and implementation process of online teaching. Online learning at Hostos is also discussed in Chap. 7.

References

Aisch, G., Buchanan, L. Cox, L., & Quealy, K. (2017, January 18). Some colleges have more students from the top 1 percent than the bottom 60. Find yours. *The New York Times*. Retrieved from https://www.nytimes.com/interactive/2017/01/18/upshot/some-colleges-have-more-students-from-the-top-1-percent-than-the-bottom-60.html?_r=0

Allen, I. E., & Seaman, J. (2015). *Grade level: Tracking online education in the United States*. Retrieved from http://www.onlinelearningsurvey.com/reports/gradelevel.pdf

Attewell, P., Lavin, D., Domina, T., & Levey, T. (2006). New evidence on college remediation. *The Journal of Higher Education, 77*(5), 886–924.

Bacow, L., Bowen, W., Guthrie, K., Lack, K., & Long, M. (2012). Barriers to adoption of online learning systems in U.S. higher education. *ITHAKA S + R*. https://doi.org/10.18665/sr.22432.

Bailey, T., Jeong, D. W., & Cho, S. W. (2010). Referral, enrollment, and completion in developmental education sequences in community colleges. *Economics of Education Review, 29*(2), 255–270.

Chen, C., & Shaw, R. (2006). Online synchronous vs. asynchronous software training through the behavioral modeling approach: A longitudinal field experiment. *International Journal of Distance Education Technologies, 4*(4), 88–102.

Chickering, A. W., & Gamson, Z. F. (1987). Seven principles for good practice in undergraduate education. *American Association of Higher Education Bulletin, 39*(7), 3–7.

Community College Research Center (CCRC), Teachers College Columbia University. (2013, April). *What we know about online course outcomes*. Retrieved from https://ccrc.tc.columbia.edu/media/k2/attachments/what-we-know-about-online-course-outcomes.pdf

Driscoll, M. (2000). *Psychology of learning for instruction*. Needham Heights, MA: Allyn & Bacon.

Freire, P. (1970, 2018). *Pedagogy of the oppressed*. New York: Bloomsbury Publishing USA.

Gautreau, C. (2011). Motivational factors affecting the integration of a learning management system by faculty. *The Journal of Educators Online, 8*(1), 1–25.

Grenslitt, J. (2018, April 25). Innovative, collaborative digital community colleges recognized in annual survey. *Center for Digital Education*. Retrieved from http://www.govtech.com/education/awards/digital-community-colleges/Innovative-Collaborative-Digital-Community-Colleges-Recognized-in-Annual-Survey.html

Holmes, B., Tangney, B., Fitzgibbon, A., Savage, T., & Meehan, S. (2001). Communal constructivism: Students constructing learning for as well as with others. In J. Price et al. (Eds.), *Proceedings of Society for Information Technology & Teacher Education International Conference 2001* (pp. 3114–3119). Chesapeake, VA: AACE.

Hostos Community College (HCC). (2017). *Strategic plan framework 2017–2022*. Retrieved from https://issuu.com/hostoscollege/docs/2017-2022-strategic-plan-framework-?e=4241348/54698225

Hostos Community College Office of Educational Technology (HCC EdTech). (2019). *Hostos online course development guidelines*. Retrieved from https://commons.hostos.cuny.edu/online/wp-content/uploads/sites/68/2018/12/Hostos-Online-Course-Development-Guidelines.pdf

Hostos Community College Office of Institutional Research and Student Assessment (HCC OIRSA). (2018). *Hostos Community College: Fall 2018 student profile*. Retrieved from http://www.hostos.cuny.edu/Hostos/media/Office-of-the-President/Institutional-Research-Assessment/rptHostosStudentProfileUpToF18_1.pdf

Jaggars, S. S. (2014). Choosing between online and face-to-face courses: Community college student voices. *American Journal of Distance Education, 28*(1), 27–38.

Kauffman, H. (2015). A review of predictive factors of student success in and satisfaction with online learning. *Research in Learning Technology, 23*, 1–13.

Kester, L., Kirschner, P., & Corbalan, G. (2006). Designing support to facilitate learning in powerful electronic learning environments. *Computers in Human Behavior, 23*(3), 1047–1054.

McQuiggan, C. (2012). Faculty development for online teaching as a catalyst for change. *Journal of Asynchronous Learning Networks, 16*(2), 27–61. Retrieved from https://files.eric.ed.gov/fulltext/EJ971044.pdf

National Center for Education Statistics. (2018, November). Enrollment and employees in postsecondary institutions, fall 2017; and financial statistics and academic libraries, fiscal year 2017. Retrieved from https://nces.ed.gov/pubs2019/2019021.pdf

National Center for Public Policy and Higher Education. (2011, June). *Affordability and transfer: Critical to increasing baccalaureate degree completion*. Retrieved from http://www.highereducation.org/reports/pa_at/index.shtml

National Student Clearinghouse Research Center. (2017). *The role of community colleges in post-secondary success: Community colleges outcome report*. Retrieved from https://studentclearinghouse.info/onestop/wp-content/uploads/Comm-Colleges-Outcomes-Report.pdf

Oh, S., & Jonassen, D. H. (2007). Scaffolding online argumentation during problem solving. *Journal of Computer Assisted Learning, 23*(2), 95–110.

Oldenburg, B., & Glanz, K. (2008). Diffusion of innovation. In K. Glanz, B. K. Rimer, & K. Viswanath (Eds.), *Health behavior and health education* (4th ed., pp. 97–121). San Francisco, CA: Jossey-Bass.

Omrod, J. (2004). *Human learning* (4th ed.). Upper Saddle River, NJ: Pearson Education.

Onwuegbuzie, A., Witcher, A., Collins, K., Filer, J., Wiedmaier, C., & Moore, C. (2007). Students' perceptions of characteristics of effective college teachers: A validity study of teaching evaluation from using a mixed-method analysis. *American Educational Research Journal, 44*(1), 113–160.

Rogers, E. M. (2003). *Diffusion of innovations* (5th ed.). New York: Free Press.

The Board of Higher Education, Office of the Dean for Community College Affairs. (1968, April). *A proposal for the establishment of community college number eight*. Hostos Library Archives.

The City University of New York/Office of Institutional Research and Assessment (CUNY OIRA). (2018). *CUNY interactive factbook: Hostos*. Retrieved from https://public.tableau.com/profile/oira.cuny#!/vizhome/CUNYInteractiveFactbook_1/FacultyProfile

Wingo, N. P., Ivankova, N. V., & Moss, J. A. (2017). Faculty perceptions about teaching online: Exploring the literature using the technology acceptance model as an organizing framework. *Online Learning, 21*(1), 15–35. https://doi.org/10.10.24059/olj.v21i1.761.

Wolfe, K. S., DiSanto, J. M., Poma, I., & Rodriguez, W. (2018). Hostos Online Learning Assessment (HOLA) follow-up: Student perceptions in two cohorts. *Hispanic Educational Technology Services Online Journal, 8*(2), 19–52.

Xu, D., & Jaggars, S. S. (2014). Performance gaps between online and face-to-face courses: Differences across types of students and academic subject areas. *The Journal of Higher Education, 85*(5), 633–659.

Where We Fit

Kristopher Bryan Burrell

Hostos Community College is committed, as are all of the colleges within the City University of New York (CUNY), to improving the socioeconomic mobility of its students. At a campus located in one of the poorest congressional districts in the country, this part of the college's mission is particularly salient. Part of Hostos' mission is to "offer access to higher education leading to intellectual growth and socio-economic mobility through the development of linguistic, mathematical, technological, and critical thinking proficiencies needed for lifelong learning and for success in a variety of programs" ("Our mission," 2018). The college has demonstrated its commitment to fulfilling its mission for students and the broader South Bronx community in various ways, including evincing an increasing willingness to invest in developing the college's technological capacity and educational technology offerings, especially over the past two decades. Among New York City residents, the student body at Hostos is particularly affected by a relative lack of broadband Internet access. As a result, these students benefit from both reliable high-speed Internet access on campus and faculty efforts to integrate educational technology into courses

---

K. B. Burrell (✉)
Behavioral and Social Sciences Department, Hostos Community College, CUNY, Bronx, NY, USA
e-mail: KBURRELL@hostos.cuny.edu

that are populated with a variety of learning styles and external constraints on time, such as full-time employment and familial responsibilities to children or older relatives.

The majority of Hostos students live in the Bronx and take public transportation to campus. The average commute of a CUNY student lasts between 45 and 60 minutes. The three subway lines that come to the college are above ground in the Bronx, presumably giving students who possess mobile phones and data plans the benefit of cellular Wi-Fi access as they ride the train to and from campus. However, on their trip, they may experience intermittent Wi-Fi access, thereby making it likely that the student will not be able to stream a video for class without interruption or review an assignment online as the signal strength will not be strong enough even along these densely populated corridors of the Bronx (HCC OIRSA, 2018).

Of the boroughs of New York City, Bronx residents have the least broadband Internet access. The Bronx has the highest percentage of households without broadband Internet throughout the entire city. Thirty-four percent of households do not have broadband Internet access. This is compared to only 21% of households in Manhattan (Smith, 2017; Stringer, 2014; Wiley, 2016). Additionally, among Bronx neighborhoods, Bronx Community Districts 1 and 2—where Hostos Community College is located—reflect the same disparity in households lacking broadband access as the borough at large. In fact, across the twelve community districts of the Bronx, in only three was the percentage of households with broadband Internet access over 70%, while across Manhattan's twelve community districts only three of those districts had access percentages below 70% (Stringer, 2014). Significantly, two of those Manhattan community districts included Central Harlem and East Harlem, the community districts in closest physical proximity to Hostos.

As a result, Hostos Community College and other public institutions like it serve a vital role in providing reliable, high-speed Internet access for students and other Bronx residents. The college and other public institutions, such as libraries, provide the necessary technological support for students to be successful, not only in school but in their lives beyond school. Figures from 2013 illustrate that, in New York City, there were higher percentages of broadband Internet subscriptions among those with employment, compared with the unemployed and those "not in the labor force;" and those with bachelor's degrees or higher, compared with those with high school diplomas or less (Stringer, 2014). Eighty-nine percent of New Yorkers with a bachelor's degree or higher have a broadband Internet subscription, while only 60% of those with less than a high school equivalency diploma have broadband. Among employed New Yorkers, nearly 84% have a broadband subscription, while among unemployed New Yorkers the percentage falls to 79% and drops even further to 66% for those "not in the labor force" (Stringer, 2014). City leaders recognize that "broadband is a necessity" for economic mobility and educational success in the twenty-first century (Wiley, 2016). And, as CUNY library faculty Maura Smale and Mariana Regalado wrote, "The importance of computer and Internet access to academic life in the 21st century is difficult to overstate. Students we spoke with were required to use computers to complete assignments that ranged from weekly reading responses and short-answer assignments to term papers" (2014). For Hostos students, as with other CUNY students, access to and proficiency with broadband Internet access, adequate devices, and relevant educational technology are critical for student success and greater socioeconomic mobility.

Hostos Community College has dedicated greater resources to the development of its technological capacity and support for communication and instructional purposes over the past two decades. Each move Hostos has made in this area has been important for its student body and has also positively impacted the broader community. However, before the year 2000, the college did not have a particularly vibrant culture of promoting the use of educational technology. In fact, Internet access was very much a luxury for the majority of students and faculty members, which limited the connection deemed necessary by Freire in *Pedagogy of the Oppressed* between foundational concepts and the ability to practice what was learned (1970). The college did not have a place where faculty could obtain support if they were interested in incorporating technology into their courses. The limitations, in terms of both Internet and device availability, and the specialized knowledge needed to utilize materials, meant that only the most intrepid faculty, who knew how to navigate computer programs or were willing to learn how to do so on their own, would have been able to innovate their courses with technology.

One of the pioneers promoting the use of educational technology among faculty was Business professor, Julio Gallardo, a firm promoter of technology and innovation since the 1980s. Gallardo, through a National Science Foundation (NSF) grant, was able to establish the Science Resource Center that included the latest computers and evolved throughout the years, eventually becoming the Academic Computing Center that he later led ("Faculty and guests," 1981). Gallardo created some of the earliest web-enhanced and fully online courses, and managed the first learning-management system (Blackboard) at Hostos. He would continue to play an important role in the creation and development of institutional support structures for faculty throughout the 2000s. The beginnings of the college's development of a department for educational technology go back to the early 2000s with the establishment of the Office of Instructional Technology (OIT) and an Academic Computing Committee (ACC) that included members of the faculty. The OIT was initially directed by Mathematics professor, Loreto Porte, who ran the office and supervised a staff comprising only part-time employees, including Carlos Guevara. Gallardo managed the Academic Computing Center for students.

The OIT received modest funding at its inception, but was born of the recognition that students needed better access to educational technology, that faculty needed more and better training about how to incorporate technology into their courses, and that the college would need to do more to keep pace with technological change as it related to higher education. The department did not have a stable budget when it was first established—cobbling funding together from various sources, including federal grant money, student technology fees, and New York State tax-levy funds. Porte was the only full-time employee, and there were three multimedia specialists. Some faculty at the college had ideas about how technology could be effectively integrated into their courses, but the necessary support structure to assess the feasibility and facilitate the implementation of their ideas was not well defined before OIT was established. The primary function of OIT in its early years was to provide technical assistance to faculty members. This office provided support through workshops on new technologies, the creation of educational applications and websites, and assistance in the development of web-enhanced and new online courses.

In this vein, Hostos created the Teaching Innovation Support Center (TISC) in 2002. For the OIT, technology adoption was at the heart of the office's mission, as was establishing relationships with early faculty innovators to pioneer the latest tech advancements in education. Through companies, grants, and purchases, OIT often acquired the latest emerging technologies in their developmental stages to evaluate the potential for implementation at the college. After the educational technology specialists explored the possible uses for solving specific problems, the second phase was to closely work with a limited group of faculty to pilot the projects before expanding them to the college community. Through TISC, faculty interested in incorporating technology into their courses implemented groundbreaking initiatives for Hostos, including the use of interactive test-review sites, the development of technology workshops for faculty, and the use of Personal Digital Assistant (PDA) devices in classes with students. So, as faculty were being asked to incorporate web-based elements into their existing courses and develop fully online courses, the OIT was available for faculty that needed support. In 2003, under the sponsorship of the Institute for School of the Future (ISOF), the office received PDA devices to explore their potential use in college classrooms. The project was developed in 2004, and piloted in Biology, Mathematics, and Nursing courses by 2005. In the Mathematics department, for example, the project consisted of using the PDA software, Quizzler, to create quizzes and practice exercises on the device itself, or in a word-processing program using specific code. The faculty then beamed the practice exercises and quizzes to students' devices. When students completed the exercises, students had immediate access to the results, and those scores were beamed back to the faculty. The handheld devices allowed participating faculty members to see individual scores, average scores, and other statistics assessing the class' performance. Students were able to do the practice exercises and quizzes anywhere, but they needed Internet connectivity to sync their devices with the faculty devices.

Even with unpredictable funding sources and a small staff, OIT was at the cutting edge of the developments occurring within the field of educational technology, as evidenced by the grants they secured, but especially within the City University of New York (CUNY) system. When CUNY began to implement its learning-management system, known as Blackboard, throughout the university around the year 2000, Hostos faculty were some of the first to receive training on how to utilize the system. Hostos was also one of the first campuses to house and maintain Blackboard on its own internal servers, which Gallardo helped to implement. Eventually, the university decided to centralize the operation and maintenance of the Blackboard system for all its campuses in 2005, but Hostos faculty and OIT demonstrated their unwavering willingness to be involved in those initiatives they saw as benefiting students and faculty through greater knowledge of and access to educational technology (HCC OAA, 2009).

Over time, OIT and the TISC continued to demonstrate their importance to the college's development and, in 2004, the college gave OIT permission to hire a coordinator and a college lab technician to help with the expansion of support services offered to faculty and students. Under a new OIT director, Dr. Carl Grindley, a decision was made in academic year 2008–2009 to merge OIT and TISC into a single department and expand its services to students. After OIT and TISC merged into one office, instructional designers started playing a more active role with the academic departments, becoming liaisons to support the needs of particular departments.

In 2010, OIT was renamed the Office of Educational Technology (EdTech). The new name was intended to reflect trends within the educational technology field and was part of the college's rebranding effort to better advertise the services the office provided. During this period of remaking, EdTech's mission was enhanced to empower partnerships and collaborations among faculty and EdTech specialists. Although still having to function with an annually fluctuating budget, the department secured more equipment to carry out its functions for faculty and students. The office went from having three workstations for its multimedia specialists and a temporary space for math tutorials to an office with cutting-edge workstations and web servers, and a room for faculty, staff, and student training.

In 2010, Hostos invested in redesigning the EdTech office space to provide a permanent space for collaboration and to foster innovation. The new space was equipped with a state-of-the-art SmartBoard, advanced computers for the EdTech specialists, and media hardware for exploration and training. The Academic Computing Committee was also renamed the Educational Technology Leadership Council (ETLC) in an effort to make the work of the EdTech office more visible to faculty. The EdTech team was better able to foster collaborative partnerships with the faculty, and the members of the ETLC had enough power to help create substantive changes with regard to the available technology on campus.

The EdTech team and members of the ETLC began to both re-envision its current programs and institute new programs. EdTech enhanced its relationships with various departments around the college and also created new ones, as it created custom computer applications for the Career Services, English, and Mathematics departments, among others (HCC OAA, 2012). During this time, a more thoroughgoing culture of valuing the potential benefits of educational technology for improving student learning was being seeded throughout the college.

The EdTech team began reevaluating and revising its faculty-training programs for the development of fully and partially online courses. Staff members noticed inefficiencies as the number of faculty that were being monetarily incentivized to undergo training was not resulting in a proportional increase in the number of fully and partially online courses actually being taught at the college. One of the big changes that was instituted during the 2012–2013 academic year was the beginning of tying faculty incentives to not just the development, but the execution of new courses. In addition, EdTech reduced the number of faculty who could receive training and course certification in a given semester to ten. Reducing the number of faculty trained made the process of earning compensation more competitive and made it easier for the EdTech staff and ETLC members to monitor the development, certification, and implementation of new fully and partially online courses. The revamped certification process was just one of many steps that helped improve the EdTech's efficacy, solidify the office's role in educational development within the college, and cement the improvement of technological innovation as a successful component of Hostos Community College's strategic plans.

In the college's strategic plan for the years 2011 through 2016, part of the college's goal for institutional infrastructure and advancement was to "make Hostos a model for the use of technology" (HCC President's Office, 2011). The work of the EdTech team over the previous few years put Hostos in a position to take advantage of additional funds coming from CUNY and other external sources for the development of educational technology and online learning. The work of EdTech and the ETLC was beginning to be recognized across CUNY and beyond. Hostos had been publicly commended by the League for Innovation in Community Colleges, as well as other organizations and colleges across the country (HCC President's Office, 2011).

In 2011–2016 strategic plan, the college set five-year goals of having all courses utilize technology, instead of the 30% figure at the time. The college also sought to identify two academic programs that could be developed into fully online programs. In order to facilitate these kinds of improvements, the college wanted to double the number of smart classrooms across the college, provide comprehensive access to online-learning support, and inform the college community that the college had access to all students via email (HCC President's Office, 2011).

The person who would head the effort to make good on the college's goals regarding educational technology was Carlos Guevara. Though he had joined the staff as a multimedia specialist in 2002, Guevara became director of the Office of Educational Technology (EdTech) in 2012, after serving as interim director since 2011. He had overseen significant expansion in EdTech, as that office finally secured enough stable institutional funding beginning in 2013 to hire more permanent staff members and more equipment for faculty and staff use.

EdTech has also benefited from the growth of information technology infrastructure across the college. Guevara gives significant credit for the increasing success of EdTech initiatives and the integration of EdTech into the strategic success of the college to the arrival of Varun Sehgal as the vice president of the Information Technology (IT) department. According to Guevara, there has been increased collaboration between the two departments since Sehgal's arrival at the college. Guevara credited the "constant improvement in the IT infrastructure and productive collaboration with the college's [Chief Information Officer, Mr. Sehgal]," as a major factor in the continued growth and success of EdTech (K. Burrell, personal communication, 2018). He points to the development of Information Learning Commons (ILC), a shared virtual space, as one example of the fruitful partnership between IT and EdTech. The ILC "works to identify and assess college-wide technology needs, and assist with strategic planning while representing the interests of faculty, staff, students, and the rest of the college community equally" (HCC OAA, 2018).

During the period of time that the ILC was active, the EdTech team collaborated more productively with other offices and departments at the college, including the Academic Learning Center, Career Services, IT, and the Hostos Library, among many others, in different and increasing ways. Representatives from these departments and from IT met regularly to discuss common issues facing each department, such as where their services might complement one another, how to eliminate redundancies, maximize limited resources, and make each department's services more accessible for students. For example, the EdTech office trained tech tutors from departments that were part of the ILC, in order to assist students in resolving a variety of different, common technical problems. These collaborations, although the ILC is not active since 2013, have helped EdTech to keep developing collaborations with former ILC members and other offices on campus.

Now, EdTech's collaborative efforts increasingly also extend beyond the college. Growing out of the CUNY Information Technology Conference that began back in 2001, as well as the Faculty Technology Day that was established at Hostos in 2005, Guevara and faculty liaison to EdTech, Kate Lyons, reached out to the other Bronx CUNY campuses—Bronx Community College (BCC) and Lehman College—and took the lead in developing the Bronx EdTech Showcase in 2013. This initiative is further explained in Chap. 6.

Members of the EdTech team, the ETLC, and now the Hostos Online Learning Assessment Task Force (HOLA) (established in 2015), have also consistently presented their research findings at local, national, and international conferences (see Chap. 16). These have included Blackboard conferences, conferences on online teaching and learning, and conferences on educational technology. Since 2009, some of the gatherings have included the CUNY Instruction Technology Conference, the Community College Humanities Association, the Hispanic Educational Technology Services (HETS) Best Practices Showcase, and the International Conference on Teaching and Leadership Excellence, and Blackboard World, to name just a few. Faculty and staff have also collaborated on several publications over the past five years in books and journals, including *Cases on Higher Education Spaces: Innovation, Collaboration, and Technology* and the *Hispanic Educational Technology Services Online Journal.* (This initiative is discussed further in Chap. 16.)

As a result of the efforts of Guevara and the EdTech team, this office has progressed a great deal since 2010, although the foundations for such development had been laid in the previous decade. The EdTech office has expanded its initiatives and purchased more equipment to better serve faculty and students. Faculty still receive training on how to develop partially and fully online courses, although Hostos no longer compensates faculty for developing and teaching in these modalities since the 2016–2017 academic year. No longer provided monetary incentives was expected to negatively affect the number of faculty who participate in the hybrid and asynchronous course initiatives on campus going forward, but, thanks to the amount of support and mentorship offered, the numbers remain similar. EdTech initiated a program in 2015, named the Lecture Capture Initiative, for interested faculty to record their class sessions for their students as an additional preparatory tool, as well as a way for students who missed class to still receive the class content (see Chap. 6). EdTech has also continued its collaborations with individual departments to use educational technology to improve student outcomes. This has been a particularly fruitful endeavor with the Mathematics department, where there has been direct cooperation since 2009. EdTech offers device-sharing services for students enrolled in Math courses. Nearly 800 students used EdTech calculators during the 2017–2018 academic year. Twenty-six course sections also integrated the Math Web App into their sections (HCC OAA,

2018). The EdTech office has also purchased additional laptops, iPads, calculators, recording equipment, and virtual-reality equipment over the past several years in order to support the acquisition and development of more educational and instructional applications for use in the classroom. EdTech has launched new initiatives each academic year, and the number of hybrid and asynchronous course sections offered have also increased each year since 2010, from 49 sections to 206 currently (HCC OAA, 2018).

Hostos is now considered a model campus for technological innovation among the City University of New York campuses and beyond. Hostos' EdTech has garnered numerous CUNY and external awards for excellence, including the CUNY Excellence in Technology Award. The Are You Ready? course received the International Blackboard Catalyst Award for Optimizing Student Experience in 2017. The Center for Digital Education has rated Hostos among the Top 5 Digital Community Colleges during the last five years. Hostos earned the top spot in 2016 and was ranked second in 2018.

When reflecting on the future of educational technology and technological innovation at Hostos Community College, EdTech Director Guevara sees a bright future for his office and the continued development of the college: "Innovation is a continuous process and what worked yesterday might not work tomorrow. We live in a constant[ly] changing society and technology especially changes even faster. I see Hostos increasing online offerings, creating new online programs, expanding the creation of active learning spaces, [including] virtual and augmented reality, and continuing to provide a safe space for faculty to take risks and innovate. Although there is a lot more to do, I know we are on the right path" (K. Burrell, personal communication, 2018).

References

Faculty and guests inaugurate NSF-funded resource center. (1981, May). *El Coqui*. Retrieved from https://academicworks.cuny.edu/cgi/viewcontent.cgi?article=1023&context=ho_arch_savehostos_pubs

Freire, P. (1970/2018). *Pedagogy of the oppressed*. New York: Bloomsbury Publishing.

Hostos Community College, Office of Academic Affairs (HCC OAA). (2009). *Annual report, Instructional Technology, 2008–2009*.

Hostos Community College, Office of Academic Affairs (HCC OAA). (2012). *Annual report, Office of Educational Technology, 2010–2011*.

Hostos Community College, Office of Academic Affairs (HCC OAA). (2018). *Annual report, Office of Educational Technology, 2017–2018*.

Hostos Community College, Office of Institutional Research and Student Assessment (HCC OIRSA). (2018). *Hostos Community College: Student profile*. Retrieved from http://www.hostos.cuny.edu/Hostos/media/Office-of-the-President/Institutional-Research-Assessment/Profile-thru-S16.pdf

Hostos Community College Office of the President (HCC President's Office). (2011). Rooted in our mission, our compass to the future. *The HCC Strategic Plan, 2011–2016, 43*. Retrieved from https://www.hostos.cuny.edu/getmedia/f556d591-5391-4137-adf0-b10cc3590ac5/HOSTOS-Strategic-Plan-2011-2016.aspx

Our mission. (2018). *Our mission*. Retrieved from http://www.hostos.cuny.edu/About-Hostos/Our-Mission

Smale, M., & Regalado, M. (2014, September 15). *Commuter students using technology*. Retrieved from https://er.educause.edu/articles/2014/9/commuter-students-using-technology

Smith, G. (2017, December 6). Without Internet, urban poor fear being left behind in digital age. *Huffington Post*. Retrieved from https://www.huffingtonpost.com/2012/03/01/internet-access-digital-age_n_1285423.html

Stringer, S. M. (2014). *Internet Inequality: Broadband Access in New York City*, Office of the New York City Comptroller, Bureau of Policy and Research (December 2014), *1*. Retrieved from https://comptroller.nyc.gov/wpcontent/uploads/documents?Internet_Inequality.pdf

Wiley, M. (2016, January 8). *Broadband city: How New York City is bridging the digital divide*. Retrieved from https://www.thenation.com/article/broadband-city-how-new-york-is-bridging-its-digital-divide/

SECTION II

A Mindful Approach to Community Building

CHAPTER 6

Inspiring the Innovators Through Professional Development Initiatives

Carlos Guevara, Wilfredo Rodriguez, and David Dos Santos
With contributions by Iber Poma

When the newly renovated space of the Office of Educational Technology (EdTech) was reopened in 2008, it was intended to be an open space for faculty to explore new technologies, and it was also intended to promote faculty to gather, network, and collaborate on EdTech projects. The space was divided into two rooms: one with workspaces for EdTech staff and a computer bank, so faculty could work individually or together with EdTech staff, asking for help as needed; the second room was more a flexible classroom, with whiteboards, a SmartBoard, and tables and chairs that could be rearranged in different configurations. With this space as a backdrop, the EdTech team set out to develop a community of faculty who would use the space. Initially, the plan was to buy new technology and let faculty borrow

C. Guevara (✉)
Division of Academic Affairs, Hostos Community College, CUNY, Bronx, NY, USA
e-mail: cguevara@hostos.cuny.edu

W. Rodriguez • D. Dos Santos
With contributions by Iber Poma
Hostos Community College, CUNY, Bronx, NY, USA
e-mail: dsantos@hostos.cuny.edu; ipoma@hostos.cuny.edu

the new items and ask the team for help as needed; however, based on the comments of the faculty while attempting this approach, it soon became clear that some faculty members wanted something more structured.

This chapter describes three hands-on technology-exploration initiatives (iPads in the classroom, lecture capture, and ePortfolios) that EdTech developed in response to the need to offer a structured approach to learn about educational technology. The participants in these three initiatives, as well as the faculty who were part of the Educational Technology Leadership Council (ETLC) and those who participated in the Online Initiative, ended up becoming what the EdTech team called the Innovators Group. This chapter also describes the Bronx EdTech Showcase, a collaborative effort among the three City University of New York (CUNY) Bronx campuses, where faculty can present their work, receive feedback, network, and learn new approaches.

iPad Initiative

> On January 27, 2010, Steve Jobs took to the stage at the Yerba Buena Centre for the Arts in San Francisco to announce Apple's latest product. The predictions from insiders said that Apple had created a tablet computer, perhaps called the iSlate or iTablet. In fact, as we now know, Apple's new gizmo was called the iPad and it looked, as rumours had predicted, like a large iPod touch. Why, asked the critics, would anybody want one? (Richmond, 2012)

Despite some of the initial and incredulous statements by critics around the world about Steve Jobs' announcement, the potential offered by this advanced technology was enormous, and soon everyone wanted to have one; companies, consumers, and, of course, educational institutions saw in iPads the opportunity to transform education. Initiatives such as the one-to-one iPad project of the Los Angeles School District emerged across the country with the hope that this revolutionary technology would help improve student participation and success. The excitement caused by Job's words, "the iPad creates and defines an entirely new category of devices that will connect users with their apps and content in a much more intimate, intuitive and fun way than ever" (Apple, 2010) the day of the announcement, caught the attention of educators who were constantly looking for ways to present learning in a more intuitive and attractive way. From the moment these devices were created, applications (apps) were developed on a daily basis—mostly consumer-based apps—and the development of education-based apps slowly expanded. As of 2018, Apple Store contains approximately 2.0 million applications ("Number of Apps," 2019).

The iPad revolution that Apple started in 2010 came to Hostos Community College two years later. The demand of the faculty was high. They wanted to explore the revolutionary new device and wanted to provide the devices to all students in their classes, although it was not yet clear how they would integrate them with the current curriculum. Faculty across departments started to request class sets of iPads without any thought on how to use them in their courses, or how bringing these new and fancy devices would help to address a particular need or change the way they were teaching. Spurred on by the excitement and the need to establish a process to integrate new technology into the classroom in a more intentional way, the EdTech team decided to explore the potential of the iPad to improve teaching and learning and established an initiative in the fall of 2012 called iPads in the classroom. This initiative consisted of two phases: the exploratory phase focused on learning the use of iPads and the exploration of educational applications, and the implementation phase focused on how iPads could be used in the classroom.

For the first phase, Hostos acquired 20 iPads through the support of student technology fee funds (money dedicated to providing technological improvements that directly benefit and have a positive impact on student support and learning outcomes) and launched a call for faculty who wanted to explore iPads and their potential to improve the way they deliver instruction. For the first iteration of this pilot program, 20 faculty members were selected to participate in this exciting initiative. Faculty were assigned to teams of two or three, received an iPad throughout the semester, received funds to purchase applications, and received full support from the EdTech team. Participants had to attend meetings designed to provide training and offer the opportunity to learn about the progress of each team, and present their work in the form of presentations and final reports. The main objective of the initiative was to give faculty the opportunity to explore the capabilities of the device, as well as the availability and usefulness of the applications for their areas of instruction and, most importantly, to reflect on the positive and negative implications of introducing and integrating these devices and apps in the classroom. It was also important to identify how these should be presented to the students and how the curriculum should be taught.

For the second phase of the pilot program (as of 2013), Hostos Community College purchased two multimedia carts, called iPads on Wheels (iPOWs), with 30 iPads on each, again through student technology fee funds. Only the faculty who participated in the first initiative were able to participate in the second phase. The iPads in the iPOWs were preloaded with apps previously requested by the faculty. The acronym iPOWs was adopted to mimic Hostos COWs (for Computers on Wheels), another popular acronym on campus for a widely used resource. Ten faculty participated in the second phase and integrated iPad apps into their curricula and used iPOWs in their classrooms. The faculty observed that their students were more engaged in their learning, participated more in the classroom, and could learn better complex concepts. Since the first iPOWs arrived in a Hostos classroom on a Tuesday morning during the 2014 semester, faculty have been constantly adopting the device. As of the spring of 2018, more than 40 faculty and 90 sections of courses have used iPads in the classroom (HCC EdTech, 2018). This initiative continued for three years with high participation and interest from faculty. During this period, a total of 72 unique faculty members participated in the program, which represents about 43% of all full-time faculty at Hostos.

Two faculty from the Department of Natural Sciences, Dr. Zvi Ostrin and Dr. Vyacheslav Dushenkov, who participated in both phases of the initiative, conducted a research study to evaluate the effectiveness of their approach, which, according to their findings, indicates that the students show higher performance and retention indicators with iPads (2015). They have presented their findings at several national conferences, including the 2015 Bronx EdTech Showcase. This initiative continued for three years with high participation and interest from the faculty.

At the end of each academic year, the EdTech team, together with the Office of Institutional Research, administers a survey to the students in the participating classes and requests for reports to the faculty that used the iPads in their courses about their experience. The feedback received from the faculty has been very positive, who indicated that they liked the different features of the iPads. Faculty acknowledged that allowing students to respond anonymously to the surveys helped to increase their participation and collaboration with their classmates. Faculty also reported that allowing students to search the web on-site helped them strengthen their writing and research skills. Finally, faculty shared that the classroom environment was perceived as a safe place to try new technologies.

An additional benefit of this initiative—one that serves as an example of the Innovations Web—was the strengthening of the community of innovators on campus. Providing new and exciting technology for the faculty to explore became a catalyst for technology adoption and productivity improvement. More faculty came to EdTech asking for iPads and other services because they had heard about the iPad pilot. The approach and structure of this pilot became a model in making informed decisions about the acquisition of appropriate mobile-learning resources and other academic technologies.

Lecture Capture Initiative

The Lecture Capture Initiative at Hostos Community College was established in 2003 to provide faculty members with the means to record their lectures and make them available to their students for further review. Recording videos and allowing students to revise them as many times as necessary, until they understand the concepts explained in class was a trend in the pedagogical use of technology. Each emerging technology presents challenges ranging from the cost and complexity of technology to the adoption by the faculty, but this did not stop the EdTech team from bringing this advance to the college.

Lecture capture gives faculty the opportunity to expand access to information shared in the classroom, and allows students who miss the class or who do not understand a particular part of the class the first time to have access to the lecture recordings at any time and look at the content as many times as necessary until they understand the concepts. Before the implementation of the lecture-capture solution, faculty needed to explain difficult concepts several times, but they may not have had enough time to stop the progress of their curriculum to repeatedly demonstrate difficult concepts that students did not understand. With this solution, students who had difficulty taking notes while paying attention to the lesson or those who had little ability to take notes would have the opportunity to supplement what they could get in class.

Lecture-capture solutions began to evolve but presented a series of obstacles such as licenses, hardware and software costs, platform complexity, and lack of automation. The initial solution required the installation of recording software in a laptop cart. This was inconvenient for the faculty because, if they wanted to use this technology, they needed to physically go to the office and be assisted by one of the members of the EdTech team. Faculty had to physically carry the cart to the classroom, make the recording, and return to the EdTech office after using it. A few years later, an improved version using a lecture-capture server allowed faculty to connect from different computers on campus. This solved the problem of multiple users at the same time, since the instructors only needed to install the software application on a laptop to be able to record videos from their offices and/or classrooms and generate a link to the recording that was then added to the Blackboard course. Although recording and publishing on the lecture-capture site was automatic, the most complex issue was editing as it required the technical expertise of the EdTech staff. These limiting factors impeded the extensive adoption of this technology. When realizing these limitations, it became imperative to identify a solution that could offer seamless automation and a better user experience. The features of the wish list for a new solution included integration with Blackboard and the ability to quickly edit and generate closed captioning for the videos. The selected solution was Panopto.

Lecture-capture technology is here to stay and has steadily increased over the years. This technology is used in various ways, from faculty recording the entire class to recording short videos of specific class content to students recording videos of their projects or particular skill exercises, such as playing the piano. In addition to all the features mentioned above, Panopto also integrates quizzes with the videos, which allows faculty to assess students' understanding of the content. The initial Panopto pilot was carried out in 2015, and the implementation of this initiative followed the same structure for the iPad initiative. During the 2017–2018 academic year, more than 60 courses, including those in Anthropology, Biology, Dental Hygiene, English, Music, and Sociology, have integrated lecture capture. The use of this platform went from 1200 unique viewers, 7000 views, and 80,000 minutes in 2016–2017 (the first year that Panopto was deployed for the entire college) to more than 2000 unique viewers, 14,000 visits, and 165,000 minutes in 2017–2018. The ultimate success in the implementation of a reliable lecture-capture solution and integration into the institution's learning-management system and infrastructure, as well as in other necessary components such as technical resources, is due in large part to the support of senior management, especially from the provost and the chief information officer (CIO) who believed in the potential of this technology to become a powerful tool to improve teaching and learning at Hostos.

Lecture capture has become an important element in the development of online courses. The online-course development guidelines, updated in 2018, include lecture capture as one of the elements of the criteria for the course to be approved for online mode. Similar to how the iPad initiative works, the approach adopted to introduce and promote the use of lecture capture at Hostos Community College strengthens the Innovations Web by providing teachers with a framework that allows time to explore new technologies in an environment that supports and recognizes risk-taking and innovation.

ePortfolios Initiative

During the last 30 plus years, ePortfolios have been defined and redefined. A consensus among many educators and experts (Barrett, 2003; Challis & Challis, 2005; Lorenzo & Ittelson, 2005) define ePortfolio as an electronic compilation of a person's (student or instructor) work during or within a defined set of time and audience, which can be used to validate the acquired knowledge as a tool for personal growth and reflection and to share personal and educational experiences.

Initially, an ePortfolio was the traditional paper portfolio converted to some kind of electronic format. Barrett (2003) described examples of how these electronic portfolios were used by students to show their work and by professionals (e.g. specialty artists) to distribute compact discs (CDs) to companies or institutions interested in their work. With innovations in technology, new ways to provide broader access to the ePortfolio were possible; the Internet provided the possibility to publish these ePortfolios in the form of a website and to give access to a wider audience. Before Web 2.0, ePortfolios were limited to pictures, scanned documents, and text to describe the individual's experience, knowledge, and abilities. With Web 2.0, new tools became available to facilitate content creation, provide access to rich media, and interact and collaborate with peers and instructors (Zhang, Olfman, & Tactham, 2007).

All these Web 2.0 tools allow students to develop a sense of ownership and to express their creativity without thinking about the technical skills. Social networks like Facebook, LinkedIn, Twitter, and Instagram are good examples of platforms that have taken advantage of these tools and have successfully engaged people in social collaboration. As Zhang et al. (2007) suggested, these new tools help foster community participation, user collaboration and support, and social learning, which have several implications on how institutions approach ePortfolios' adoption.

ePortfolios have been replacing the traditional paper portfolio of previous decades and offer a higher purpose in postsecondary education, especially at the community-college level. They provide a convenient and relevant method to reflect and showcase the work throughout the curriculum. The ePortfolios, like the previous paper portfolios, are most frequently used on this campus in Education and Digital Design. These fields traditionally require some method of demonstrating skill and talent beyond the curriculum. In addition to a showcasing platform, the ePortfolio also serves as a reflective medium when the student reviews several drafts on the journey to the final product that will be published to the public. ePortfolios also have a vital role in the professional world: for example, applicants seeking an initial teaching position or teachers presenting credentials in application for tenure, as kindergarten through 12th-grade teachers often require a portfolio to showcase the ability to plan lessons, document continuing education, and share letters of reference. In the field of digital design, an ePortfolio serves as an indicator of skill level and artistic style. This is valuable when interviewing for a design company or to obtain clients and collaborators while working independently. The designers have been using third-party commercial ePortfolios since the infancy of the Internet.

Hostos Community College has been exploring the implementation and adoption of ePortfolios since 2008 and followed the steps of ePortfolio pioneers at CUNY's LaGuardia Community College. Throughout this process and with the technological limitations of the time, the EdTech team explored several solutions in order to provide a user-friendly platform. Platforms such as SAKAI (https://sakaiproject.org), Wordpress (www.wordpress.com), and Learning Objects (https://learningobjects.com) were explored and piloted, but the learning curve was steep and the required technical knowledge was high. After exploring emerging solutions, Hostos started to use the Digication platform (www.digication.com), a simple-to-use ePortfolio platform designed primarily for use as an educational tool that has been widely adopted by several CUNY campuses. The Digication platform comes with a pre-made template, and users are given the ability to edit the existing template or to create one themselves. No web design or programming experience is required; the platform uses a drag-and-drop editor similar to Squarespace (www.squarespace.com) and other modern web platforms. The browser-based platform has low system requirements so that even a half-decade older personal computer or laptop should be able to run the website.

The end goal of an ePortfolio is career advancement, whether that career is professional or academic. Students use their ePortfolios when applying for senior colleges and jobs. The most active faculty using ePortfolios have often heard about the ePortfolio Initiative through other professors, from the EdTech team's email blasts, and at professional development workshops. The team also targets specific departments through an internal marketing campaign to get as many faculty members on board as possible. Some faculty transform their assignments or create new ones of their own accord to fully utilize ePortfolios, while others consult with the EdTech team's instructional designers to come up with ePortfolio assignments. Faculty will then introduce the pedagogical side of the ePortfolio to their students.

ePortfolio workshops at Hostos start with introducing the end-goal potential of the ePortfolio. Workshops are approximately one hour of technical how-tos for working on the ePortfolio. Students also have the additional resource of the ePortfolio website with links to written and video tutorials of the Digication platform in case they need to review topics from the workshop. In addition to the online-support website, the EdTech team provides ePortfolio support on a walk-in basis. The office is open to both students and faculty during normal business hours as well as extended evening hours in order to facilitate evening courses and students who work during the day.

Several institutions have expressed difficulties encountered in the process of implementing a wider adoption of ePortfolio, and Hostos is no exception. Challis & Challis outlined key requirements to achieving the full potential of ePortfolios, which are not only from the technical point of view, but also from those of the student, instructor, and administrator (2005). She outlined a very important point that has to be taken into consideration to gain wider acceptance from students—students need to see that ePortfolios are part of their careers, not just as an additional assignment. They have to find the value for their program and understand its purpose. Another important point is that students need to develop a strong sense of ownership, which means that they will be able to use it beyond their academic years. These recommendations resonate with the ones offered at the Making Connections National Resource Center founded by LaGuardia Community College to the Hostos faculty team that participated in one of their programs. One of the outcomes of this participation was the creation of the ePortfolios Implementation Committee (EPIC) at Hostos in order to establish strategies to institute the key requirements cited by Challis. This committee consisted of an interdisciplinary group of early innovators eager to promote the use of ePortfolios in their departments and the college as a whole. Their work contributed to having over 1500 students using ePortfolios in more than 60 course sections every semester for the last few years.

Opportunities for Sharing: The Bronx EdTech Showcase

The Bronx CUNY EdTech Showcase, held annually toward the end of the spring semester, promotes and highlights the innovative uses of technology that have the potential to reach new levels of student engagement leading to improved performance. The three Bronx CUNY colleges (Bronx Community College, Hostos Community College, and Lehman College) began organizing this event in 2013 as a great opportunity for networking, collaborating, sharing technical information, and building upon effective practices within the CUNY community and beyond. The Bronx EdTech Showcase is a unique event and one of the few CUNY borough-wide collaborations that brings together colleagues from these three campuses and beyond to illustrate their commitment to exemplary teaching and learning in the asynchronous, hybrid, and face-to-face environments. Hostos faculty and staff members regularly present here, often as a stepping-stone to larger conferences. The administration of each of the three campuses contributes to the funding of the event; over the years, the organizing committee has been able to secure additional funding through corporate sponsorships.

On-campus events had been historically hosted to encourage faculty innovators at Hostos to share about their uses of technology in the classroom. This event was similar to events organized at other colleges from the CUNY system, where the main target population was their own faculty. In 2001, CUNY created the CUNY IT Conference, which serves as a space for faculty and information-technology professionals to share their work to an audience that is typically composed of faculty and staff from the university. This conference continues to be a great venue for faculty from all campuses to present to and learn from other colleagues.

One of the limitations from the perspective of highlighting and motivating Hostos' innovators and early adopters was that only a few presentations could be accepted at this conference, leaving few opportunities for promoting adoption and culture change at the campus level. With this in mind, and recognizing that other colleges were also struggling to offer spaces for collaboration, recognition, networking, and sharing innovations, Carlos Guevara (EdTech director at Hostos) and Kate Lyons (faculty liaison at Hostos) reached out to colleagues from the other two Bronx CUNY community colleges, Albert Robinson (assistant director of the Center for Teaching, Learning, and Technology at Bronx Community College) and Allyson Vogel (director of online learning at Lehman College), with the idea of creating a unified professional development day. Each campus already had such an event and shared similar challenges: limited resources and attendance, limited exposure to different practices/innovations, and limited collaboration and networking. Everybody was on board, and, taking advantage of the geographical location of the three campuses, the Bronx EdTech Showcase was born in 2013.

The first edition of the Bronx EdTech Showcase in 2013 was organized by the Office of Online Education at Lehman College, where an audience composed of representatives from 18 colleges within the CUNY community was exposed to the ideas, experiences, and perspectives of 57 presenters throughout the day. The Center for Teaching, Learning, and Technology at Bronx Community College hosted the showcase in 2014 with over 200 participants from 20 colleges from CUNY and beyond, and the Office of Educational Technology at Hostos Community College hosted the third iteration of this showcase in 2015 with a similar number of participants. This conference rotates the hosting campus, and, as of 2018, six editions have been celebrated, and over 1000 attendees have engaged in networking and professional development during 150 presentations and 12 keynote/enlightenment sessions.

On December 4, 2014, this initiative received the Innovation/Outstanding Project Collaboration/Service Collaboration Award at the CUNY Excellence in Technology Awards Ceremony in recognition of its innovative and collaborative effort among CUNY campuses.

The goal of this initiative, as well as of all artifacts created in the Innovations Web, is to provide faculty and the members of the institutions a venue to share and showcase the work, successes, and learning experiences that result from taking risks, being early adopters, and taking the necessary steps to become change agents. It also provides a network and a community of practice where a cultivation of support helps in the creation of a safe space to try new things and take risks. The team that now consists of Albert Robinson and Mark Lennerton from Bronx Community College, Olena Zhadko and Steve Castellanos from Lehman College, and Lyons and Guevara from Hostos Community College continues to look for new ideas to offer an innovative and engaging showcase every year.

Findings

The implementation of a structure that centers around support, community building, and promoting a safe environment to take risks has been the differentiating factor in accomplishing faculty buy-in and creating opportunities for continuous improvement that lead to increasing student success. Data analyses done by the Office of Institutional Research have shown very positive passing and completion rate indicators for the last few years since these initiatives were created with the aforementioned structure. For instance, the analysis of data from the 2017–2018 academic year shows (HCC EdTech, 2018) that the tech-enhanced courses (courses that use iPads, lecture capture, ePortfolios, or are asynchronous or hybrid) had a 62.52% passing rate in fall 2017 compared with the 54.70% passing rate of non-tech-enhanced courses—a difference of 7%. Similarly, tech-enhanced courses also show a 7% higher completion rate compared with non-tech-enhanced courses (68.19% compared with 60.65%). The data from spring 2018 show even better indicators—17% higher passing rate on the tech-enhanced courses compared with the courses that were not tech-enhanced (67.84% vs. 50.15%), and 22% higher completion rates on the tech-enhanced courses compared with the courses that were not tech-enhanced (77.64% vs. 54.45%).

In conclusion, it is important to indicate that there are several factors that impact these indicators; however, the positive gains in the passing and completion rates give us an indication that the technological improvements in the courses contribute in part to this achievement. When promoting the change in the organizational culture, it is important to take into account all the elements that have an impact and identify the appropriate ways to nurture the positive elements and turn the negative ones into opportunities. This is how the Innovations Web works and how the initiatives described in this chapter were conceived and structured.

References

Apple. (2010). *Apple launches iPad* [Press release]. Retrieved from https://www.apple.com/newsroom/2010/01/27Apple-Launches-iPad/

Barrett, H. (2003). *Electronic portfolios*. Retrieved from http://electronicportfolios.com/portfolios/encyclopediaentry.htm

Challis, D., & Challis, D. (2005). Towards the mature ePortfolio: Some implications for higher education. *Canadian Journal of Learning and Technology/La revue canadienne de l'apprentissage et de la technologie, 31*(3), Canadian Network for Innovation in Education. Retrieved from https://www.learntechlib.org/p/43166

Dushenkov, V., & Ostrin, Z. (2015). Pedagogical aspects of using mobile devices in the biology classroom. CUNY Academic Works. Retrieved from https://academicworks.cuny.edu/ho_conf_bet15/1

Hostos Community College, Office of Educational Technology (HCC EdTech). (2018). Annual report, Office of Educational Technology, 2017–2018, 8.

Lorenzo, G., & Ittelson, J. (2005). An overview of ePortfolios. *EDUCAUSE Learning Initiative, 1*. Retrieved from https://library.educause.edu/~/media/files/library/2005/1/eli3001-pdf.pdf

Number of Apps Available in Leading App Stores as of 3rd quarter 2018. (2019). Retrieved from https://www.statista.com/statistics/276623/number-of-apps-available-in-leading-app-stores/

Richmond, S. (2012, March 16). IPad: How Apple started a tablet revolution. Retrieved from https://www.telegraph.co.uk/technology/apple/9147868/iPad-how-Apple-started-a-tablet-revolution.html

Zhang, S. X., Olfman, L., & Ractham, P. (2007). Designing ePortfolio 2.0: Integrating and coordinating Web 2.0 services with ePortfolio systems for enhancing users' learning. *Journal of Information Systems Education, 18*(2), 203–214.

CHAPTER 7

The Online Learning Initiative: Training the Early Adopters

Jacqueline M. DiSanto and Carlos Guevara

According to Wolf (2006), there are four requisite components to effectively preparing faculty to teach online. Participants should have a modicum of technological skill, there must be active administrative support, faculty must be motivated, and the end product of the training should be a specific course. An earlier study had identified factors that impacted whether or not an instructor made an effort to teach online (Betts, 1998). These factors suggest that in order to motivate an instructor to attempt an online course, faculty require information regarding online education, they may need proof that the quality of instruction will not be less than in a completely face-to-face course, they want an opportunity to discuss experiences with colleagues, and they would like their opinions to be heard in a safe environment.

J. M. DiSanto (✉)
Education Department, Hostos Community College, CUNY, Bronx, NY, USA
e-mail: jdisanto@hostos.cuny.edu

C. Guevara
Division of Academic Affairs, Hostos Community College, CUNY, Bronx, NY, USA
e-mail: cguevara@hostos.cuny.edu

© The Author(s) 2019
K. S. Wolfe et al. (eds.), *Developing Educational Technology at an Urban Community College*, https://doi.org/10.1007/978-3-030-17038-7_7

Introduction

The office of Educational Technology (EdTech) at Hostos Community College implemented the asynchronous and hybrid initiatives during the 2009–2010 academic year. This purposeful, constructive approach to professional development was intended to introduce new faculty to online education by providing comprehensive training with the explicit goal of increasing the number of sections offered in an online modality.

Original efforts to motivate faculty new to online teaching fell short of the desired outcomes. Workshops were offered by highly competent faculty and staff; however, information about what an online course looked like and the benefits of making online sections available to students did not generate the desired results. Although faculty attended the workshops and appeared interested in the information presented, there was not a noticeable increase in either the number of faculty willing to create an online section of a course or in the number of sections available to students.

Bohlen and Beal (1957) used their 1957 diffusion process model to address adapting to and using new technologies, and Bohlen and Beal (1957) assigned each sociological group an attitude toward new technology in their technology-adoption lifecycle: (a) Innovators (influential, eager to be first to try); (b) Early Adopters (practical, their support can lead to the success of those who follow); (c) Early Majority (willing, need some support); (d) Late Majority (skeptical yet obedient, will follow after others have been successful); (e) Laggards (resistant, will try when faced with no other alternative). Selecting a focused group of participants and working with them until they are successful and able to serve as an example to others is an excellent way to "bridge the chasm" (Moore, 1991, pp. 7–14) that exists between those who are willing to try and those who are extremely reluctant.

By considering models such as the technology-adoption lifecycle to identify a target group of potential participants, a purposeful initiative to train faculty to create and teach online course sections was formed. The rationale was that faculty would be able to design an online course and be able to deliver instruction using the online platform if they had one-on-one guidance as well as widespread support. It was anticipated that this support would originate within the academic department with the promise of scheduling the new online course and assigning it to the designer to teach the following semester and that faculty mentors and EdTech specialists would provide tutelage in the requisite pedagogical and technical skills needed to provide instruction online.

THE HOSTOS ONLINE INITIATIVE

Online learning at Hostos Community College is defined as "courses that are delivered through either the hybrid modality, or the asynchronous modality," and online instruction occurs through Blackboard (HCC EdTech, 2018). Asynchronous courses typically do not meet in person; instead, delivery of instruction occurs completely online. In hybrid courses, between 33% and 80% of the instruction must be given online with the remaining time spent in face-to-face class sessions. One possible way to allocate the time in a hybrid section is to take the face-to-face schedule offered, which typically consists of two in-person class sessions (a class session at Hostos is equivalent to 75 minutes), and simply divide it into two. One face-to-face session each week remains; the other class session is dedicated to online instruction.

In order to increase the number of courses offered online across the different content areas and to sustain the increased number of offerings beyond the initial semester it is taught, it was decided to develop a comprehensive training program so that faculty would feel confident that they had the ability and tools necessary to teach a course from the first day through the final exam. An assessment approach was used whereby a panel of experienced online faculty would review each new section to determine whether it was viable and ready for students. These reviewers were widely recognized as innovators and early adopters in online instruction.

Forming the Cohort

The creators of the initiative focused on a mentor-mentee platform (rather than a top-down format) where the teacher seeking training would work with a colleague with tri-level experience in (a) adapting curriculum to either an asynchronous or hybrid format; (b) delivering instruction using the Blackboard platform; (c) engaging students in the online environment. Furthermore, it was decided that the ultimate goal was the successful running of a newly developed online course—not just its creation. The invitation to participate was sent to all faculty across the academic-content areas. It was anticipated that colleagues from within a unit or department would encourage others to join but also that there would be buy-in from a wider, campus-wide perspective.

These partnerships would be part of a community of practice (Schein, 1992, 2004, pp. 25–38) supported by multiple departments and divisions across campus. Among the offices providing assistance to participants and setting the standards by which each proposed online course is assessed are as follows:

1. Educational Technology (EdTech), which develops, implements, supports, and promotes innovative integration of technology into teaching and learning by empowering faculty, serving students, and creating a supportive environment for all types of learners. EdTech provides instructional design and technological assistance (https://commons.hostos.cuny.edu/edtech/about-edtech/);
2. EdTech Leadership Council (ETLC), charged with monitoring and evaluating campus educational technology policies and procedures and making recommendations when needed, and whose members promote the use of educational technology within their respective departments and advocate for technology needs (HCC OAA, 2018) (see Chap. 8).

Additionally, unit coordinators and department chairs would assist in identifying a course to adapt to the online environment and agree to both schedule the course and assign the developer to teach it the next semester. Student-support offices such as Academic Advisors and Success Coaches would share information about the newly created online section with students.

The EdTech staff and ETLC work hand in hand to inform academic faculty about best practices and to provide support for faculty seeking to expand their use of technology to deliver online instruction. This includes working with instructors as they develop the technical skills necessary to actually teach in an online environment. EdTech extends the initial call for participants before the beginning of each new cohort of online course developers.

There are several roles faculty can assume in the initiative. They can develop an asynchronous or hybrid section of a course that has never before been taught online, or they can be trained to teach an online section that had been developed by someone else and had already been taught. They could also be asked to serve as a mentor if they had successfully created and taught an online section for several semesters. Developers could be tenure-track faculty, lecturers, or instructors, and could be full-time or adjunct faculty.

Those faculty interested in participating in the initiative were asked to apply and had to identify a course that would be adapted to the online environment. Permission had to be obtained from their department that included assurance that the new section, once approved, would be scheduled to run the following semester.

Participants were required to share their work and meet with their mentors throughout the semester. The mentor's responsibility was to offer practical and pedagogical guidance and recommendations based on personal experience and best practices, while allowing the mentee to craft a course that reflected individual expertise and preferences. The assumption was not that it was a leader-follower relationship, but one of mutual interest in advancing online learning across campus and of reciprocal respect. It was not unusual for the mentor to gain enhanced technological skills or gather new resources during the initiative.

Structure

Faculty were required to begin with an existing syllabus, complete with student-learning objectives, common or equivalent assignments, and anything else that was a non-negotiable component of the existing course. Attendance at a series of meetings was compulsory throughout the semester. These were facilitated by different people who were invited to share their expertise in a specific area relevant to online instruction.

The initial meetings focused on the different components of a well-crafted online course, particularly as it would appear to students. Faculty were provided with a shell course to use as a template for designing their online center. For those participants who had never taken an online course or even attempted to use Blackboard as a resource in a face-to-face course, designing the actual layout of the course took time and practice. Items that were non-negotiable and needed to be added to the shell included the syllabus, textbook information, student-learning objectives and program-learning outcomes, schedule of topics with tests and assignments, grading policy (including how the final grade is calculated), faculty contact information, and an open line of communication.

The first point of emphasis shared with new participants was that the online version of the course had to remain true to the course description as written in the college bulletin. Student-learning outcomes and any other parts of the course that are required by the department for all sections such as the textbook, a common assignment, and grading policy had to be included. By maintaining the integrity of the course from its initial design, the stage was set to have an online section be as effective as a face-to-face one.

The second caveat from the beginning meeting was that student engagement is key to the success of an online course—as it is in face-to-face sections. Faculty received training on using the announcement function to maintain frequent contact with students; announcements allow students to sense the instructor's presence by receiving reminders about deadlines, finding out about events taking place on campus, or simply being told words of encouragement. They also received assistance crafting discussion forums that entice students to showcase what they learned by sharing their personal takeaway or reaction to a topic. Discussions are also an excellent way to have students develop relationships, albeit invisibly, with classmates and to receive informal feedback from the instructor.

Once faculty started to fill in the different components in the course shell, the meetings addressed less specific topics. One session provided an overview of learning styles and helped faculty connect the different aspects of an online course that would work with certain types of learners and also identify areas that some students would find unappealing or difficult to use. For example, a student who is not task persistent might find that working with an instructor who is not physically present wreaks havoc with the ability to complete assignments. In this case, the instructor could help by sending deadline reminders and posting them clearly in multiple places such as the syllabus and assignment directions.

Faculty frequently raised questions about administering quizzes and tests online. Timing the exam, maintaining fairness, minimizing cheating, and grading the answers were all valid concerns. Faculty were reassured that there is no right or wrong way to do this online, and the mentors worked one-on-one with their colleagues to help each personalize how they wanted the testing experience to be in their class. EdTech staff demonstrated how to create a quiz, test, or assignment on Blackboard and how to organize and maintain a virtual gradebook.

Additional topics included creating resources such as videos or podcasts, using team-based learning in an online course, and holding online office hours. The EdTech and ETLC staff and faculty were prepared to address questions from the cohort as needed.

Mentor-Mentee Relationship

Faculty who were developing courses were expected to attend all meetings and to meet with their mentor regularly. Mentors were volunteers and were frequently paired with a colleague based on common academic specialty where both worked in the same unit or department; they both may have even taught the course being developed. In some instances, colleagues were paired outside of their academic-content areas based on past history of working well together.

Innovators

Between fall 2011 and spring 2015, mentors were culled from the online innovators on campus. These were the people who used Blackboard, many times even in classes that did not require online instruction. Perhaps they used it as a class repository for documents, articles, directions, and so on or perhaps they used it as a communications tool between class sessions. They were enthusiastic and did not need convincing that creating an online course was a good thing to do. They viewed it as necessary because students would need to be able to find, retrieve, and use information once they begin their careers.

Recruitment was not limited to the emailed invitation. Often innovators personally spoke to people with whom they had worked closely on a committee or special project. Their enthusiasm and their first-person account of how they went from novice to actually teaching online was often the aha-moment that pushed an as-yet unconvinced colleague to attempt the initiative.

Mentors were asked to offer guidance and to serve as a sounding board for concerns and questions. It was not intended for the course of the mentor to be replicated in their mentee's shell. Listening is one of the essential ways a mentor can be of assistance to their colleague. Considering the opinions and teaching styles of a person with whom they are working and helping them arrive at a way of presenting information that suits how *they* teach motivates a new-to-online instructor to remain involved in this new modality (Betts, 1998).

Early Adopters

Faculty who joined the initiative in order to create an online course between fall 2011 and spring 2015 were paired with innovative colleagues who had previously created online sections either independent of any formal program or who had gone through the original series of workshops before teaching online. These new participants were enthusiastic and often reported being motivated by the success of a colleague or the idea of trying something relatively new.

Academic freedom was another area of interest for the early adopters. Being able to present information to students in a different venue than the physical classroom as well as being able to design that venue to be current and to have the ability to update content easily by adding online resources are reflective of real-world work environments. Students often come to class with the ability to find up-to-the-minute information on their cell phones or tablets, and many have adequate to advanced technological skills. Arranging course content and designing assignments, particularly research, in an online classroom may help engage students who are bored with static, printed resources.

For those early adopters who were confident that they would be able to successfully develop and teach an online course, mentorship was often a future goal. For this online initiative to be successful, it needed to expand in the number of courses offered and the number of people involved. It was accepted by all that having a mentor work with more than one or two people in a given semester would not be effective. The initiative was not only preparing more people to create and teach online, it was preparing more people to serve as future mentors.

Mutual Benefits

The mentor-mentee relationship was not the only connection established in each group. Discussions took place at meetings where attendees shared their own experiences and preferences outside of their designated role in the initiative. Everyone had the opportunity to hear the successes and challenges of others and to seek advice from someone whose work they admired.

By engaging in pedagogical dialogue, all participants had the opportunity to enhance their own course. All were respected as valued contributors regardless of their technological skills or experience teaching online. No one's opinion or story was inconsequential; everyone had a voice at the table simply because of their shared dedication to online learning.

There was financial compensation for both the mentee and the mentor. The initiatives were grant supported during the early-adopter phase, and compensation was structured in two increments for the person creating the new online section. The first amount was paid once the section was approved as an online section; the second amount was paid at the end of the first semester it was taught by the person who created it. The mentor was paid after the section was submitted.

Reaching the Early Majority

As the online initiative was solidifying after spring 2015, there was the need to rethink and establish a more sustainable approach from the economical and support perspectives. Although, initial grant funds allocated to pay stipends to developers and mentors ended, the institution was committed to providing the necessary support to ensure that online learning continued to grow. Also, with the expansion of online courses throughout the City University of New York (CUNY), the development of these courses started to be seen as part of the regular professional responsibility of faculty. Cognizant of the importance of recognizing the additional work and commitment from faculty that is necessary to develop quality online courses, the EdTech team redefined the online initiative to establish a strong support system to help the developer throughout the process. Starting in fall 2015, dedicated faculty mentors and instructional designers were assigned to each developer. Also, a three-module, six-hour self-paced online course, Roadmap to Teaching Innovation, was developed and deemed a requirement of the online initiative. Although there was a concern that faculty would not want to participate due to the absence of stipends, the creation of a very robust support structure has helped to maintain a steady number of participants in the online learning initiatives.

Final Product

Developers must have completed their shell by a specified date near the end of the semester and received their mentor's approval before it could be submitted to the panel for final review. The EdTech team in collaboration with the EdTech Leadership Council (ETLC) crafted the development guidelines for hybrid and asynchronous courses (HCC EdTech, 2015), which replaced the previous guidelines that were created a decade ago and which have since gone through several revisions. EdTech and ETLC worked to ensure that the current guidelines were based on emerging national standards and best practices, such as the rubrics developed by California State University (CSU) Chico and Quality Matters. Among the criteria considered are as follows:

1. Was it appealing to the eye and well organized?
2. Did it have all of the required components?
3. Was there an initial announcement welcoming students to the course?
4. Was the instructor's contact information listed, including office hours and email?

5. Were the directions and due dates for assignments clear and easy to read?
6. Were the different policies (grading, academic integrity, etc.) readily available?
7. Were directions available for different functions such as online discussions?
8. Was the course content accessible and developed by applying universal design concepts?

There were basically three responses that a developer of a submitted course received. Course shells were approved as is, approved with some revisions, or held for major revisions. As it was a condition of being accepted to the initiative, faculty who created an approved online course were expected to teach it the following semester.

Success

There are several factors that contributed to the success of the Online Learning Initiative at Hostos Community College. The first is that one of the largest groups of new faculty began working at Hostos in fall 2012, right in the middle of the early-adopter phase of the initiative. EdTech has always worked very closely with the campus's Center for Teaching and Learning (CTL), which provided the year-long, new-faculty orientation as well as a rigorous schedule of professional-development activities for all faculty and members of the college community. Several online innovators served on the advisory council to CTL and helped present different topics to the new faculty. By developing collegial relationships early on, many of these newcomers quickly applied to the initiative during their second and third years of teaching here.

The second supporting factor was an act beyond anyone's control—Hurricane Sandy—also in fall 2012. At least five days of classes were canceled due to the storm, which left many unable to come to campus for numerous reasons. It was decided that individual class sessions would be made up online. As not everyone knew how to do this, training was set up with academic faculty and EdTech staff who were comfortable using Blackboard and who held workshops for colleagues to help them design and upload their compensatory classes.

One determinant of the success of the Hostos online initiatives is the increase in the number of *different* courses offered in each of the online

7 THE ONLINE LEARNING INITIATIVE: TRAINING THE EARLY ADOPTERS

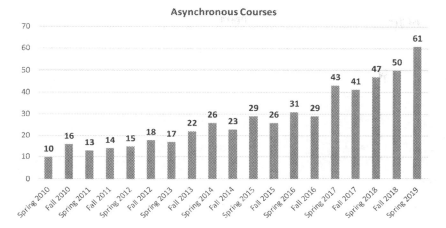

Fig. 7.1 Growth in asynchronous courses

modalities. Prior to the start of the initiative in fall 2011, the number of courses offered asynchronously averaged 13 each semester. After the initial initiative, that number began to rise in spring 2012 where 15 asynchronous courses were offered and dramatically expanded over the next 14 semesters despite the elimination of stipends (see Fig. 7.1). In the spring 2019 semester, 61 courses were offered.

The number of hybrid sections offered (see Fig. 7.2) increased by more than 230% between spring 2011 and spring 2015—from 24 courses to 56. There were 73 sections offered in fall 2018. One possible explanation for this was discussed by Garnham and Kaleta (2002), who offered flexibility as a possible explanation for increased interest and participation in hybrid courses (as cited in Lloyd-Smith, 2010, p. 510).

At this urban, highly diverse community college, students assume numerous roles each week—learner, employee, parent, caretaker, and volunteer. Faculty must follow a rigorous professional path toward tenure and promotion that includes teaching, service on committees, conducting research, and publishing, and must also meet their personal responsibilities.

Teaching hybrid courses allows faculty the opportunity to make the most of the limited hours each week by giving them the freedom to prepare their online sessions at a time that is most convenient to them. It also

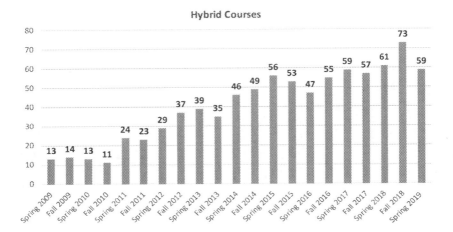

Fig. 7.2 Growth in hybrid courses

gives them expanded time to consider student questions and requests compared with feeling the need to respond more immediately in person.

The different courses offered also grew in variety across multiple departments. By spring 2013, courses were available in many of the degree programs and academic-content areas. The percentage of hybrid and asynchronous courses offered increased from 2.3% (25 courses) in spring 2010 to 12.1% (120 courses) by the start of spring 2019; the total number of individual courses offered in this modality rose by 480% (see Fig. 7.3).

The growth illustrated in Fig. 7.3 is a concrete measure of the success of the online initiatives. It is highly likely that the innovators and early adopters on our campus motivated the early majority to attempt online teaching because of their modeling the user-friendliness of the initiative, the effectiveness of teaching in an online modality, and the collegial support provided by EdTech and the mentors. In recent cohorts, it has been often noted that faculty suggest colleagues within their program or department for the next initiative, rather than individuals signing on independently during the pre-initiative workshop training.

As the participants in the online-teaching program at Hostos Community College progressed from innovators and early adopters to the next sociological groups of early- and late majority (Bohlen and Beal, 1957), the increase in the number of online courses continued to escalate.

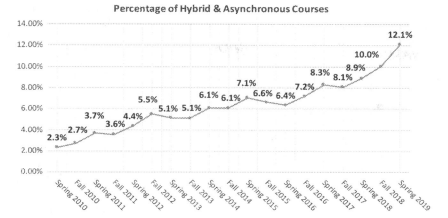

Fig. 7.3 Growth in percentage of hybrid and asynchronous offerings

Course offerings for the fall 2018 semester spanned 24 academic-content areas; there were 50 asynchronous sections and 73 hybrid sections for which students could register. This steady growth during all these years has positioned Hostos Community College as one of the principal leaders of online learning at the City University of New York as reflected on the 2017–2018 university performance-management process (PMP), where Hostos has the highest (9.1%) percentage of instructional (student) full-time equivalencies (FTEs) offered partially or totally online among the CUNY community colleges, and the seventh highest among all CUNY colleges (CUNY, 2018).

Beyond Success

The increasing number of online courses offered at Hostos, while laudable, has created new challenges in ensuring that students in online courses report the same or higher levels of satisfaction and experience similar academic success as students in traditional face-to-face courses. While scaling-up has been challenging, the organizational culture and foundational community encouraged by the EdTech team, as well as the continued support from senior administration, have been fundamental for managing through the scaling-up hurdle. The establishment of the Hostos Online Learning Assessment (HOLA) task force (also discussed in Chap. 16), which promotes assessment and a culture of continuous improvement, and the work of the EdTech Leadership Council (ETLC) have resulted in a complete revamping of the guidelines for online in course development in 2018, which offer a more granular approach and guidance to developers and evaluators (HCC Online, 2018). These guidelines were influenced by national standards and best practices together with the addition of other emerging comparative measures such as the Open SUNY Course Quality Review (OSCQR), adopted by the Online Learning Consortium (OLC).

Another result that derives from the work of the task force is the reformulation of how students are prepared for online learning. Results from the online-student perceptions study showed that it was crucial to create a more robust orientation and training for students who were interested in or enrolled in online courses. The creation of the Are You Ready? online student-readiness course (see Chap. 11) helped to address those needs and to streamline student support for online learning. Additionally, the college may soon need to establish guidelines for using open-educational resources (OERs) as this college has rapidly been expanding its course offerings that use OERs (see Chap. 12).

As the number of online courses continues to increase and planning for the development of online programs begins, there is a need to restructure the way online learning support is managed and to establish a stronger structure to assist faculty, students, and support offices. With the approval of the administration, Guevara created the online learning unit within the Office of Educational Technology and hired an online learning coordinator and two additional part-time instructional designers to help establish necessary protocols and policies, as well as to extend the hours of operation for nights and weekends to better meet the needs of those involved in online learning at Hostos.

When observing how online initiatives have evolved during this decade, it is important to highlight that one of the determining factors for their successful results has been the ability to connect all the dots and ensure that each one fed and guided the other. This has been a crucial mechanism for organizational culture change and innovation. Online learning initiatives follow the Innovations Web framework (see Chap. 3) to continue making improvements, establish the necessary support structures, and engage the community of innovators. Although there is still much to be done to expand and sustain online learning at Hostos, the EdTech team has a strategy for the future.

References

Betts, K. (1998). An institutional overview: Factors influencing faculty participation in distance education in postsecondary education in the United States: An institutional study. *Online Journal of Distance Learning Administration, 1*(3). Retrieved from https://www.westga.edu/~distance/ojdla/fall13/betts13.html

Bohlen, J. M., & Beal, G. M. (1957). The diffusion process. *Agricultural Extension Service, Iowa State College Special Report, 18*(1), 56–77.

CUNY. (2018). *Performance monitoring data book: 2017–2018 university report.* Retrieved from http://www2.cuny.edu/wp-content/uploads/sites/4/page-assets/about/administration/offices/oira/institutional/data/current-student-data-book-by-subject/PMP_University_Data_Book_2018-Final_2018-08-16_v4.pdf

Garnham, C., & Kaleta, R. (2002). Introduction to hybrid courses. *Teaching with Technology Today, 8*(6). Retrieved from https://hccelearning.files.wordpress.com/2010/09/introduction-to-hybrid-course1.pdf

Hostos Community College Office of Academic Affairs (HCC OAA). (2018). Retrieved from http://www.hostos.cuny.edu/Administrative-Offices/Office-of-Academic-Affairs/Information,-Policies,-and-Guidelines/OAA-Committees

Hostos Community College Office of Educational Technology (HCC EdTech). (2015). *Hostos Hybrid and Asynchronous Course Development Guidelines.* Retrieved from https://commons.hostos.cuny.edu/online/initiatives/

Hostos Community College Office of Educational Technology (HCC EdTech). (2018). *About EdTech.* Retrieved from https://commons.hostos.cuny.edu/edtech/about-edtech/

Hostos Community College Online Learning (HCC Online). (2018). *Hostos Online Course Development Guidelines.* Retrieved from https://commons.hostos.cuny.edu/online/wp-content/uploads/sites/68/2018/12/Hostos-Online-Course-Development-Guidelines.pdf

Lloyd-Smith, L. (2010). Exploring the advantages of blended instruction at community colleges and technical schools. *Journal of Online Learning and Teaching, 6*(2), 508.

Moore, G. A. (1991). *Crossing the chasm: Marketing and selling high-tech products to mainstream customers* (Rev. ed.). New York: Harper Collins.

Schein, E. H. (1992). *Organizational culture and leadership* (2nd ed.). San Francisco: Jossey-Bass.

Schein, E. H. (2004). *Organizational culture and leadership* (3rd ed.). San Francisco: Jossey-Bass.

Wolf, P. D. (2006). Best practices in the training of faculty to teach online *Journal of Computing in Higher Education, 17*(2), 47–48.

CHAPTER 8

Reaching Beyond the Innovators

Kate S. Wolfe

The theory of innovation that has guided the work here at Hostos has indeed followed the model that includes early adopters of innovative technologies and pedagogies as well as middle and late adopters (Rogers, 2003). Many of this book's contributing authors were early adopters, such as Professor Sandy Figueroa and Dr. Jacqueline DiSanto. They have become leaders in our college community as peer mentors and role models for our community of practice. They have also served formally as mentors in the online-learning initiative. These faculty are engaged in developing best practices in pedagogy as well as technology. They have built online courses that offer students scaffolded assignments, group work, and more individualized attention than what may be common for first-and second-year college students. These faculty believe in preparing students for future careers and college transfers. This leads to their emphasis on technology as a means of social mobility. Thus, students at Hostos are better prepared to bridge the digital divide that exists in the South Bronx because of the efforts of early adopters and the support offered by the Office of Educational Technology (EdTech).

K. S. Wolfe (✉)
Behavioral and Social Sciences Department, Hostos Community College, CUNY, Bronx, NY, USA
e-mail: kwolfe@hostos.cuny.edu

Many faculty are followers in the middle of the adoption curve. In fact, the number of faculty using Blackboard in their pedagogy at Hostos has increased greatly since 2009. Some faculty are late adopters, coming on board when they observe the success of their colleagues. And some, at least so far, are never adopters—faculty who would never teach online, despite their facility with other forms of technology. This chapter will now look at the organizational structure at Hostos and the means of information dissemination used since Carlos Guevara became director of Educational Technology.

Organizational Structure

CUNY Academic Technology Committee (CAT)

This university-wide committee is comprised of representatives from each campus as well as CUNY (City University of New York) Computing and Information Services (CIS), the University Faculty Senate, and the CUNY Office of Academic Affairs. Meetings are held monthly, and its standing committees also meet monthly on topics such as Blackboard, Online Learning, Library Technology, and the CUNY Academic Commons.

Departments

Departmental structure at Hostos varies. Some departments have chairs and deputy chairs (e.g. Math and English), while others have chairs and unit coordinators (e.g. Behavioral and Social Sciences, and Education). Other departments such as Natural Sciences have course managers. Therefore, decisions about online-course development vary greatly. Some departments will not approve adjuncts to undergo asynchronous or hybrid course development training. In order to create online (asynchronous or hybrid) courses, all courses must be approved by department chairs because newly developed courses must be taught the semester immediately following approval. Complicating matters is the fact that the Office of Academic Affairs (OAA) is currently requesting faculty schedules almost a year ahead of when they will be taught. Courses that are approved in December for the spring semester then must be added to the course schedule at the last minute. Also, this structure seems to allow people not to participate in technology initiatives. Some faculty may not have had the desire to join the EdTech initiatives and they have always had the ability to opt out.

Office of Educational Technology (EdTech)

A reimagining of programming in the Office of Educational Technology began in 2010. EdTech members strengthened relationships across the entire campus and created new computer applications for various departments like Advisement, Athletics, Career Services, English, and Math. This was the inception of building a culture that values student success and seeks to improve student learning across campus.

Additionally, members of EdTech are visible participants in key committees on campus, thereby giving them voting rights on important academic issues. This presence and each person's input into discussions on curricular items underlines the mutual benefits that occur when different agencies within a campus work together by sharing perspectives and energies. Currently, members of EdTech are members of the college Senate and serve on its Elections and Instructional Evaluation committees (HCC OAA, 2018a).

COLLEGE-WIDE COMMITTEES

Educational Technology & Leadership Council (ETLC)

This committee, previously known as the Academic Computing Committee, is "charged with monitoring and evaluating campus educational technology policies and procedures and making recommendations when needed, and whose members promote the use of educational technology within their respective departments and advocate for technology needs" (HCC OAA, 2018b). It was renamed the Educational Technology & Leadership Council (ETLC) to increase collaborative relationships and visibility among faculty, and also to more clearly reflect the functions and purposes of the committee as the role of technology has changed dramatically since the founding of the committee. This committee was established in the fall of 1994 and directed to serve as an advisory body to the vice president of academic affairs in matters that relate to educational technology. The ETLC has members from every department, most of whom have taught in either the asynchronous or hybrid modality. Current faculty liaison Kate Wolfe is the chair of the ETLC, and serves with co-chair Carlos Guevara. Other members represent the Allied Health, Business, Education, English, Humanities, Language and Cognition, Library, Math, and Natural Sciences departments. This committee has helped create changes in terms of academic technology on campus. The ETLC works with EdTech to plan and promote professional-development initiatives and activities for faculty and students, approve online courses, explore new technologies, and inform the university community about the role and importance of technology in improving teaching and learning.

New Asynchronous Guidelines
ETLC assumed the task of reimagining the checklist used to approve asynchronous and hybrid courses that were developed through the online initiatives (see Section II, Chap. 7). ETLC supported the EdTech team to revamp the former course development guidelines that had been last updated in 2015 to provide developers and evaluators a more thorough and granular set of guidelines.

Peer Observation Improvement Network for Teaching (POINT)

The Office of Academic Affairs established the Peer Observation Improvement Network for Teaching (POINT) in 2011; it was comprised of faculty from different academic departments. However, it did not include any participants from EdTech until Guevara became the co-director of the Center for Teaching and Learning (CTL), a position he fulfills while also serving as director of EdTech. POINT was then assigned to be part of CTL. POINT's goal was to disseminate best practices in peer observation with the intent to provide a point of reflection that could ultimately lead to a more effective pedagogy (HCC OAA, 2012).

This committee has created guidelines for conducting faculty observations in hybrid courses based on those created for asynchronous courses more than ten years ago by an instructional evaluation committee. POINT remains part of CTL, which provides professional development to support faculty in the improvement of their pedagogical practices in all learning modalities. POINT has developed criteria that showcase how peer observations function in an online environment. Observers evaluate delivery of content as well as how the faculty member uses specific online tools to facilitate student learning and engagement. Assessing teaching must be consistent and rigorous no matter the modality in which the course is taught. These new guidelines help put online and hybrid courses on par with so-called traditional courses that are held in a face-to-face setting, and they emphasize that teaching in the online environment is valued just as much as in the physical classroom by the college's personal and budget committees and campus decision-makers (HCC OAA, 2018c).

OUTREACH AND DISSEMINATION EFFORTS

Newsletter

EdTech's newsletter, *EdTech Innovations,* which is published in print and digital format with a new issue published each semester, disseminates information on news, services, and innovations, as it seeks to build relationships across campus, within CUNY, and in the education field in general. This newsletter serves to increase the visibility and awareness of EdTech's services among the academic departments.

Individual faculty are invited to write an article discussing a project they have successfully implemented, an aspect of online instruction in which they have a degree of expertise, or an event where they were a participant. This authorship, although not peer reviewed, can still support professional growth by giving faculty a way to share resources, research findings, and practices with their colleagues, thereby contributing to the field of online education. This newsletter article serves a purpose and may be a bridge to a scholarly article; it communicates valuable information with others doing similar work, and the reaction the author receives from their like-minded peers may inspire the expansion of the newsletter into a submission to a scholarly journal. Olson (2010) stated that "of the three typical kinds of service – community service, institutional service, and service to the profession – the first one is the least valued in a university setting, and the last one is the most valued" in assessing the accomplishments of faculty in higher education. Busy faculty may not have time to attend faculty-development activities but they may be able to read a short article in the newsletter, which may encourage them to give something new a try.

The creation of *EdTech Innovations* was inspired by a need to increase awareness of EdTech services on campus and improve communication about technology news and events. Prior to the newsletter, EdTech information was distributed through the EdTech website, flyers, posters, and emails sent through the distribution list; these media are still used. As effective as they are, however, the number of faculty using Blackboard and attendance at EdTech workshops had reached a plateau. The EdTech team decided that a hard-copy publication delivered directly to faculty would be a proactive way of attracting interest and participation and should increase those numbers.

Awards

Hostos has been recognized nationally as the leading, number-one digital community college in the nation by the Center for Digital Education in 2016, was listed as in second place in 2018, and had been listed among the top five in the previous years. The EdTech team has also received various CUNY Excellence in Technology awards for the numerous projects and initiatives that have been developed throughout the years and received the International Blackboard Catalyst Award for Optimizing Student Experience in 2017. It has been a long but successful process of organizational culture change at Hostos.

Innovation Chase and Innovation Celebration

The Innovation Celebration began in 2013 as a way to create spaces for dialogue around technology and pedagogy, to try out new resources like virtual-reality glasses or TWINE, and to celebrate those who participated in EdTech activities and those who used different technologies like iPads most often with prizes and awards.

Introduced in 2014, the Innovation Chase was Hostos' unique way of recognizing technological innovation by Hostos faculty. This chase consists of digital badges that can be earned by faculty and which represent their ability to use and show expertise in new technological or pedagogical approaches. This game-based learning approach encourages participation and some constructive competition among faculty. Each badge has points associated with it that help faculty see who the top innovators at the college are, as each accumulates points for their innovations (see Chap. 9).

Presentations and Dissemination of Achievements

Guevara and the EdTech team often present at national and international conferences about the work and achievements of EdTech (Guevara, 2019). The Bronx EdTech Showcase is also a way to disseminate the work of the EdTech team and faculty innovations (see Chap. 6). Presentations are done at different college-wide venues in an effort to disseminate the results of the different initiatives and research studies conducted by the EdTech team to the college community. For example, Guevara and Wolfe presented at a meeting of college chairs, coordinators, and directors detailing the results of research conducted by the Hostos Online Learning

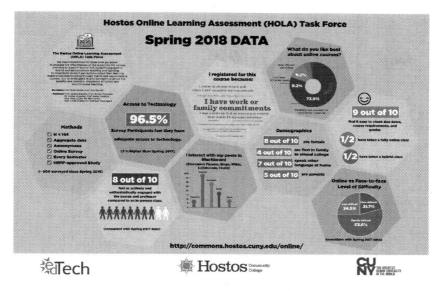

Fig. 8.1 Student perceptions of online learning – Spring 2018 data

Assessment (HOLA) task force since 2015 (see Chap. 16). The following infographic was created by the EdTech team in order to disseminate the most current results of the survey of student perceptions of online learning (Fig. 8.1).

Collaborative Efforts

When Guevara, the director of EdTech, was asked to also manage CTL in 2015, there was a unique opportunity to have more structured and intentional collaborative efforts between CTL and EdTech. The ubiquitous nature of technology presented the opportunity to rethink how technology was perceived and approached and to apply the concept of using technology as an enabler to take teaching and learning to the next level. This has resulted in improved productivity and effectiveness by establishing a common calendar of professional-development activities and promoting collaboration in the creation of initiatives such as Teaching Day, Day Zero, CTL Spa Day, Hostos Reads, Hostos Authors, among others, which highlight the perfect integration of technology and pedagogy. Similarly, the various faculty-inquiry groups that fall under the auspices of CTL, including those focused on digital literacy, peer observation, the scholarship of teaching and learning, service learning, and team-based learning, have incorporated technology as part of their conversations and, most importantly, have developed strong collaborations with EdTech and CTL. These two offices have also benefited from being viewed as extensions of each other. EdTech and CTL are in a unique position to learn from and provide support to each other as they seek to successfully conduct their initiatives and projects.

Conclusion

Guevara and the EdTech team emphasized encouraging faculty to embrace the following values: risk-taking, community-building, and innovation. These were important for building an organizational culture that would promote the adoption of educational technology. Change engages people on a psychological level, evoking both positive and negative reactions. Faculty have to go beyond their comfort zones, which is something they ask students to do in their courses. Therefore, the EdTech team created a safe environment for risk-taking, community-building, and innovation. Students are non-traditional, often have children and other family responsibilities, and often are underprepared, so to have courses that are more accessible and flexible was an important consideration in adopting these values.

Being innovative meant implementing new technologies and new teaching practices, often before best practices had been established. Faculty and staff did the work by developing those best practices when adopting innovative technologies and pedagogies. They had to engage in trial-and-error learning and had to be unafraid to fail in that process. Failing may be daunting to many new faculty so often early adopters are experienced faculty who are willing to experiment. For a small community college short on resources, the EdTech team had to encourage faculty not to wait on other developing best practices for new learning technologies. Faculty had to take on the role of researchers in order to determine the efficacy of adopting these new practices.

Hostos faculty and the EdTech team have excelled at embracing these values. Hostos has been nationally recognized as a leader among the digital community colleges since 2016. As is evident, the EdTech team has devised new and innovative ways to communicate the research being conducted as well as the work within the online-learning, iPad, and Lecture Capture initiatives. The Innovation Chase and the Innovation Celebration recognize the top innovators at the college and encourage collaboration and engagement in the EdTech initiatives.

Hostos reaches out within the college community, across the broader university, and to the external academic community in other ways, too, as a means of encouraging reluctant faculty to participate and of sharing the great work the EdTech office is doing. The newsletter published every semester disseminates information on innovations and helps build the visibility of the EdTech office and team. The newsletter offers faculty an opportunity to write short articles, see what others are doing, and discover who is working on something similar. A short article may ultimately lead to a scholarly peer-reviewed article.

The dissemination of the work and achievements of the EdTech team and faculty at conferences, college meetings, and forums along with the collaborations between the CTL team and faculty-inquiry groups are crucial to strengthen the community of innovators and recognize their efforts to innovate and improve student success.

All of these initiatives and efforts help inform the college, CUNY, and academia what a small community college in the South Bronx can do. This college wins awards in digital technology, remains innovative, and inspires others across CUNY and within Hostos. These dissemination efforts demonstrate the importance of connecting the elements of the Innovations Web in order to continue to serve as a leader in establishing best practices in online education, conducting research, and maintaining collaborative relationships.

References

Guevara, C. (2019). Carlos Guevara ePortfolio – Profession. Retrieved May 23, 2019, from https://hostos.digication.com/carlosguevara/profession

Hostos Community College, Office of Academic Affairs. (2012). Annual report, Office of Educational Technology, 2010–2011, 3.

Hostos Community College Office of Academic Affairs (HCC OAA). (2018a). *College-wide senate standing committees.* Retrieved from http://www.hostos.cuny.edu/Administrative-Offices/College-Wide-Senate/Standing-Committees

Hostos Community College Office of Academic Affairs (HCC OAA). (2018b). *Committees.* Retrieved from http://www.hostos.cuny.edu/Administrative-Offices/Office-of-Academic-Affairs/Information,-Policies,-and-Guidelines/OAA-Committees

Hostos Community College Office of Academic Affairs (HCC OAA). (2018c). *Reappointment, promotion and tenure.* Retrieved from http://www.hostos.cuny.edu/Administrative-Offices/Office-of-Academic-Affairs/Information,-Policies,-and-Guidelines/Personnel-Budget

Olson, G. A. (2010, October 17). How we value faculty work. *The Chronicle of Higher Education.*

Rogers, E. M. (2003). *Diffusion of innovations* (5th ed.). New York: Simon and Schuster.

CHAPTER 9

Celebrating the Innovators

Kate Lyons

Meehan, Rigby, and Rogers (2008) identified communication and celebration as key steps that organizations can take to build and influence their organizational cultures. They wrote, "People want to feel excited about the future and rewarded for making progress toward it, so creating appropriate incentives is important" (p. 5). With this in mind, starting in 2013, the EdTech team committed to building excitement on campus and decided to try ideas that would celebrate and reward those who adopted both educational technology and the values the office wanted to espouse (risk-taking, community-building, and innovation). The office tried two tactics—organizing Innovation Celebrations for each semester for those working with educational technology, and creating Innovation Chase, an online badges game. Those who accumulated the most points in the Innovation Chase received prizes and were recognized as Hostos top innovators at the biannual Innovation Celebration. As described in the college's annual report:

> EdTech hosted two Innovation Celebration events this academic year, where 74 faculty members participated in highly interactive round table discussions. These events were the perfect opportunity to recognize the

K. Lyons (✉)
Hostos Community College, CUNY, Bronx, NY, USA
e-mail: clyons@hostos.cuny.edu

© The Author(s) 2019
K. S. Wolfe et al. (eds.), *Developing Educational Technology at an Urban Community College*, https://doi.org/10.1007/978-3-030-17038-7_9

College's top innovators, all of whom received an EdTech Innovator customized tumbler as a token of acknowledgment and recognition. These events in conjunction with all the other initiatives offered this academic year contributed to an increment in the number of faculty using technology in comparison with the fall 2013 semester. (HCC EdTech, 2014)

Change theorists Higgins and McAllaster (2004) described cultural artifacts as "those sets of attributes – objects and behavior – that help definitively characterize one organization as opposed to another" (p. 64). They then referred to the five types of cultural artifacts identified by management theorist Paul Shrivastava as "key values and norms; myths and sagas; language systems and metaphors; symbols, rituals and ceremonies; and the use of physical surroundings including interior design and equipment" (Higgins, 2004, p. 64). Changing the cultural artifacts in the organization can drive change, and therefore, as the EdTech team looked to organize the celebrations and the rewards-and-badges game, they tried to identify places in those initiatives where culture was transmitted through those artifacts and they tried to ensure that the culture transmitted aligned with the values they wanted to espouse. This chapter discusses the planning and execution of the Innovation Celebration and the Innovation Chase Game, the two initiatives meant to celebrate success, particularly in the context of Shrivastava's five types of cultural artifacts (Higgins & McAllaster, 2004).

Background

By the spring of 2013, a group of early EdTech adopters was solidifying and growing; the office wanted to thank and recognize this group and ensure their continued commitment to using technology in their teaching. Many of the faculty members who had been teaching online since the inception of online learning (and/or using technology in face-to-face classes) at Hostos remained committed to online learning as EdTech's leadership transitioned to Carlos Guevara. The institutional knowledge contained within this group, along with their long-standing connection to the college, was invaluable and thanking them for their perseverance was sincerely heartfelt. Making this gratitude public for the other faculty and staff members at the college was important, as their risk-taking and innovation took both bravery and time commitment; this effort deserved recognition.

This early group was also key to bringing in others on campus who might be interested in joining EdTech initiatives. By the end of the 2012–2013 academic year, 43% of courses were made available on Blackboard. Eighteen courses used ePortfolios across the following disciplines: Business, College Orientation, Criminal Justice, the CUNY Language Immersion Program (CLIP), History, Dental Hygiene, Digital Design, English as a Second Language (ESL), and Visual and Performing Arts (HCC EdTech, 2013). Most departments were represented on the EdTech Leadership Council (ETLC), and iPads were reserved 104 times for classes (HCC EdTech, 2013, 2014). By 2013 the innovators' group seemed well established, and the buzz about EdTech was starting to move on to early adopters.

The year 2013 was not only a time when the group of early adopters and innovators on campus was beginning to solidify, but it was also a time when pundits were questioning the future of a brick-and-mortar education. Foursquare and Facebook were popular, and iPads, which were released just three years earlier in 2010, were all the rage. App development was acutely prolific, and new projects (especially in social media) were popping up everywhere. Many education professionals saw opportunities to use these new technologies to improve teaching and learning. At that time, Kevin Ducoff in a *Huffington Post* article named 2U (which offers online degree programs by partnering with universities), EdSurge (connects entrepreneurs with educators), Echo360 (develops tools for online learning), Noodle (search engine for topics in education), and Always Prepped (online tool for managing student and classroom data) to be the companies they "expect will impact higher ed" in 2013 (2012). Massive Open Online Courses (MOOCs) were also gaining significant traction. James Mazoue, writing on Educause, a popular media outlet for educators, described the disruptive power of MOOCs as nearly certain: "There is compelling reason to think that unbundling institutional knowledge provision and credentialing is not only gaining momentum but is inevitable" (2013).

As momentum for online learning was increasing at Hostos, it was also escalating at CUNY overall. Notably, the creation of Participatory Online Open Courses (POOCs) was started at CUNY, as Jessie Daniels described in a post on the Just Publics 365 project blog. She described the reason for creating POOCs as, "We wanted to create something participatory, rather than massive. Something that engaged with people outside the academy, as well as with those inside" (2013). This excitement about online learning that was starting to spread at other CUNY campuses was an important ingredient for building excitement at Hostos. The CUNY Academic Commons (https://commons.gc.cuny.edu/), an online collaborative space for the entire CUNY community, was just a few years past its initial launch. There were additional ways in which the Hostos community connected with other CUNY campus communities; one example was cross-campus committees and conferences. The popular attitude in 2013—that online education would eventually replace in-person higher education—was spreading to CUNY, and many of our faculty and staff members felt that excitement.

At Hostos the EdTech team overheard faculty talking about the buzz about online learning, especially about MOOCs and POOCs, in informal spaces such as in passing during committee meetings and in hallway conversations. Regardless of their prior connection to the EdTech team and technology, whether strongly for or strongly against, it seemed like there was a group emerging at Hostos that wanted to talk about how they were hearing that technology was changing education. The EdTech team realized the need for setting aside time to talk about the predicted disruptions in education and the approach to online learning that other institutions—both within and outside of CUNY—were taking,. The EdTech team was also enjoying the growing confidence, as their efforts to increase technology adoption were starting to work. It was time to productively celebrate success with an energy-generating event, and thus the idea of Innovation Celebrations was conceived. Although it was initially a moment to recognize the innovators group and offer time to talk about the increasing momentum for online learning, the EdTech team mindfully considered details about the event that would transmit the organizational culture they wanted to espouse to all faculty and staff on campus, as everyone was invited.

Across five years of Innovation Celebrations from 2013 to 2018, the structure of the Innovation Celebrations changed multiple times. All, however, offered participants significant time to talk about their experiences using educational technology, the opportunity to use new applications or hardware, and a segment for awards, when those who participated the most in activities and trainings and those who used educational technology the most often (and used the most types of technology, such as teaching with iPads, teaching online, using lecture capture, using ePortfolios) would receive prizes. Also, each celebration started with remarks from Guevara and sometimes from the co-director of the Center for Teaching and Learning (CTL) and leaders in the Office of Academic

Affairs (OAA). The provost frequently gave opening remarks at the event. The provost's and OAA's presence has been a significant way to communicate to the campus that their work in educational technology is meaningful and appreciated by the campus leaders.

Because of the success of Innovation Celebrations and inspired by the growing popularity of badging games like FourSquare (www.foursquare.com/) and Mozilla open badges (www.openbadges.org), the EdTech staff was motivated to bring the idea of rewards and celebrations a step further, and so began the Innovation Chase game in Fall 2014. The EdTech team used Wordpress (www.wordpress.org/) and the open-source WordPress plugin, originally Achievements. Eventually they switched to the BadgeOS Wordpress plugin (www.badgeos.org), which connects to Credly (www.credly.com) and allows for external use of badges (e.g., it allows faculty to connect the badges with their LinkedIn profiles). The EdTech team created a leaderboard page on their WordPress server, which also hosted, in addition to the EdTech site, those of the Hostos Library, CTL, and other offices on campus. Faculty members who earn the most points in the Innovation Chase game received prizes at the Innovation Celebration. The Innovation Chase website describes how this initiative encourages and celebrates the group of innovators:

> Each semester we celebrate our campus EdTech Innovators – everyone who's using technology to explore new pedagogical approaches. We applaud you for being the first, for developing best-practices yourself (because maybe you're doing something nobody else has). For the epic win, innovate in the most EdTech categories and (most importantly!) help your colleagues level up. The ultimate award will be yours. (HCC EdTech, 2018)

The badges give faculty members a path for trying new ideas and participating in projects. For example, faculty members can earn participation badges by attending the annual Bronx EdTech Showcase or by attending workshops organized by either CTL or EdTech. Workshop topics might be about technology or teaching, and often include presenters from other departments, including academic departments and the library. Faculty members can also earn expert badges when they participate in activities that demonstrate strong knowledge about particular topics, including Blackboard, ePortfolios, Lecture Capture, Mentoring and Mobile Learning. When faculty members see the possible badges to be earned, they are also looking at new ideas for incorporating technology into their teaching.

The EdTech team discusses the Innovation Celebration each semester, including the structure of the event, the prizes, and the badges in the Innovation Chase game with members of the Educational Technology Leadership council (ETLC). As ETLC is a steering committee for the EdTech team, with representatives from each of the departments on campus, it is a key group of faculty that advises the EdTech on how to reach out to their colleagues. ETLC, along with the EdTech, plans aspects of the Innovation Celebrations and Innovation Chase game in the context of questioning how cultural artifacts can help them find opportunities to affect organizational culture and drive change.

Key Values and Norms: Encouraging Collaboration

Although the EdTech staff was not consciously guided by the behaviors and norms found in "The Agile Way of Working," a framework for describing teamwork, this model closely resembles the values and norms of the EdTech team. Krehbiel et al., for example, described the "importance of collaboration over individual accomplishment . . . As faculty, we should facilitate meaningful group interactions requiring engagement, cooperation, and contributions from all. We believe that a collaborative approach generally produces better results than any individual could have achieved alone" (2017, p. 97). Although using this approach to teamwork was not intentional because this concept was originally for software development, it may be that the EdTech staff, even subconsciously, modeled the type of teamwork they learned from their past educational and professional experiences. Regardless, the value of teamwork, in tandem with the cooperation and meaningful group interactions that accompany it, the demand for individual responsibility to the rest of the team, and the need for individuals to be confident enough to share their ideas and work and receive feedback, is central to the EdTech Office.

In planning and organizing the Innovation Celebration and in the development and management of the Innovation Chase game, these values and norms are transmitted from the EdTech team to members of ETLC. The planning documents for the events are all co-written using Google docs (https://www.google.com/docs/about/), which means co-authors have to be willing to have their words edited, erased, and changed, and they have to feel confident changing the work of their teammates. ETLC members all accept roles in the Innovation Celebration—greeting people, facilitating discussions, sharing their experiences with new technologies, tweeting as the event occurs, and so on. While individuals are celebrated and awarded during the ceremony, a sense of teamwork permeates the event.

Sharing lessons learned is also a key value of EdTech. It is a value that benefits faculty, as sharing information through scholarship is also needed for reappointment, tenure, and promotion, and benefits EdTech and the college as it improves the reputation of the department and the school. The Innovation Celebration is an opportunity for faculty to present their experiences informally and receive feedback before submitting their works to conferences and/or for publication. Because faculty can use the Innovation Chase leaderboard to see which other faculty members are working in their same areas (like online learning, ePortfolios, etc.), this and the Innovation Celebration are also a way to match faculty to others who are learning about similar EdTech tools and pedagogical innovations.

Using Myths and Sagas to Encourage a Culture of Community-Building

In a 2005 speech to the National Center for Healthcare Leadership, Jim McNerny, Chairman and Chief Executive Officer of the Boeing Company, described how "in a super-competitive world, no one has the luxury... if that is what it is... of allowing any of their people to leave their brains at the door" (McNerney, 2006) and used a story to drive home the point. He tells the audience, "One of the (true) stories that have passed into GE lore is the hourly worker who told Welch, 'For 25 years, you paid for my hands when you could have had my brains – for free'" (2006). His story and the message he transmits—the need for everyone to be engaged, learning, and improving—resonate with the EdTech team's values. However, it is the way McNerney couched his lesson in a story, one he described himself as having passed "into GE lore" (2006) that makes his message memorable and gives people a story to retell. This retelling is an effective way to transmit the values of an organization.

The Innovation Celebration is a time when attendees are encouraged to tell each other stories about their experiences with using technology in their teaching. One of the ways the team structured the celebrations was to guide attendees through a series of ice-breakers using iPads with NearPod (www.nearpod.com). Each person at the event had an iPad logged into a NearPod presentation, and the facilitators would send slides, prompts, and activities to all the iPads. Using NearPod, attendees could provide feedback to the group, through which the facilitators could then selectively share their individual answers or the aggregate responses to activities like polls and quizzes. ETLC generally worked together with the EdTech team to come up with prompts; this usually involved asking attendees to find others at the Innovation Celebration who had done something like taught online or used ePortfolios, for example, and then share their stories with each other. As small teams, they would then turn those stories into pictures or summarize them, send them back to the facilitator through Nearpod, and finally the facilitator would share these with the large group. Though most of those stories did not make it into the team's lore, members of the EdTech team have received some references to these events repeatedly in other contexts at the college.

Using Language Systems and Metaphors to Transmit Perseverance and Opportunity

Higgins and McAllaster (2004) described language as a cultural artifact. They wrote:

> The language systems and metaphors used in organizations portray the organizations' values. Organizations develop their own language for expressing who they are and what they are about. Some companies want to 'kill the competition,' or 'battle the enemy.' Other companies use the language of the technologies they use; for example, software writers sometimes talk about an issue being on their 'heads up' display. (p. 70)

The language used by EdTech reflects that their main goal is achieving measurable outcomes set by the institution's strategic plan primarily through faculty, staff, and student development. The language is motivational and collaborative, rather than competitive. It is the language of persuasion.

When the group first began organizing the Innovation Celebration, they discussed the vocabulary to use on the flyer and decided on pitching the event as fun. One of EdTech's challenges is that faculty and staff are pulled in so many directions, with so many competing activities and tasks, that getting their attention and ensuring attendance at an event can be difficult. The EdTech team originally considered calling the event a "party" or a "meeting" but decided that "celebration" did the best job of highlighting the successes of the innovators by recognizing that there is something and some people to celebrate. Because the team had labeled a particular group as "innovators" and wanted to communicate that the EdTech team values innovation, including that particular word in the title was a unanimous decision. Describing the event as fun on the flyers and advertising the event as a place to talk with colleagues in an informal atmosphere were successful. Attendance at the Innovation Celebration has consistently been higher than at many of EdTech's other events and trainings.

Generally, the language at Hostos reflects the teaching mission and is motivational. Hostos students face many obstacles (especially financial, academic, and health issues) to their success and need to have the grit and perseverance to persist despite setbacks. *Finding opportunities, celebrating success,* and *persisting* are the words and phrases highlighted at meetings with students throughout the college. It is the language that keeps people going. Innovators, those who are trying to use a new practice rather than integrate a well-documented best-practice, are also a group more likely to experience failures and challenges. The motivational turns of phrases most often repeated at Hostos are the same ones that could inspire the Innovators group.

BADGES AS SYMBOLS OF APPRECIATION

Changing lesson plans, learning new technology, and reflecting on teaching practices is time-consuming, and there is no guarantee for faculty that the time spent will reap positive results. The college's culture effectively rewards success through reappointment, tenure, and promotion, but not necessarily through the effort that goes into being at the front of innovation, where best-practices are developed but not yet determined, and thus failure is more likely. One of the EdTech team's goals was to celebrate this work. Also important was transmitting to the faculty in the college who had not yet adopted any strategies for teaching with technology that their attempts would be similarly appreciated and rewarded. Although these faculty members might see flyers inviting them to the Innovation Celebration and they might know about the Innovation Chase website, they also might not attend Innovation Celebrations and might not ever visit the website to learn about the EdTech opportunities on campus. The EdTech team decided that physical symbols of the

Innovation Celebration as well as digital symbols such as icons, consistent design, and graphics would be a way to catch the attention of the faculty who are not early adopters and remind them of EdTech's presence on campus.

Physical symbols for the Innovation Celebration and Innovation Chase game came in two main forms—buttons to distribute at the celebration and branded prizes. EdTech used a button-making machine to create physical badges for faculty who leveled up and earned badges for each achievement in the Innovation Chase. Faculty members wore these physical pins at the celebration and around campus. Generally, the idea of faculty members carrying physical symbols around campus seemed well-received; however, the logistics of creating all the small buttons was challenging and not sustainable. The buttons broke too quickly and fell off participants' bags, jackets, and so on. More durable physical symbols were needed and so began the idea of awarding prizes printed with logos.

The EdTech team offered three types of prizes during the celebration. The first two were related to the Innovation Chase game—participation prizes for faculty members who attended the most training and participated in the most initiatives over the course of the semester and mastery prizes for those who mentored others and/or turned their learning into action, like teaching online, using lecture capture, and integrating the videos into Blackboard,. Third, the EdTech team hosted a raffle so that some of the people who attended the Innovation Celebration but were new to EdTech would also have a chance to win prizes. The prizes were all imprinted with the Innovation Celebration logo and were generally items that faculty and staff members might carry around campus, like water bottles or items symbolic of technology such as USB-drive bracelets, power bricks, or USB-powered lights.

Finally, the celebrations featured purposefully festive food. For example, one year there was a cake decorated as a tablet device. Another year the cake was printed with the Innovation Celebration logo. The logo and the digital icons that represented each badge in the Innovation Chase were also symbols. Each badge represented a type of technology, and most looked like award ribbons. The icons were consistently used for all branding and marketing of the EdTech events and training and were also designed to communicate the ideas of fun, success and celebration.

Creating a Learning Organization Through Celebrations

Learning can happen anywhere. Professional development need not be confined to designated workshops and classroom-style events. The EdTech team, while they saw the Innovation Celebrations as just that—celebrations—they also recognized the opportunity to turn them into faculty development sessions, though they were never marketed as such.

The first Innovation Celebrations focused on discussion tables and traditional, short presentations from faculty members who talked about their use of technology in the classroom. Round table discussions were a way for participants to learn from each other, but they did not model using any EdTech tools. In the next iterations of the event, the EdTech team began bringing iPads to the celebration and used NearPod to lead attendees through games and groupwork. As a result of modeling group-discussion facilitation with NearPod, a few of the Innovation Celebration participants wound up developing new lessons for their classes that took advantage of the iPad app. The EdTech team has also brought cardboard Virtual Reality (VR) viewers so that participants could watch demos on using VR in the classroom. Bringing technology to the celebration was a chance to practice what EdTech preaches.

One year, the Innovation Celebration galvanized a series of brown-bag lunch discussions. The EdTech team noticed which topics attendees at the Innovation Celebration continued to discuss, the ones that most seemed to engage them, and organized lunch chats so they could continue the conversation later. Somewhat controversial topics like "Should your students be allowed to use their phones and tablets in your classroom?" and "What can I do to reduce cheating when students are taking exams online?" attracted as many as twenty to thirty faculty and staff members for each brown-bag discussion.

Senge (2006) explained the need for workers to be able to see the whole of an organization rather than just their job and then described the "learning organization" as a place "where collective aspiration is set free, and where people are continually learning how to learn together" (p. 3). Innovation Celebrations, which bring people together to celebrate, communicate, and create an experience together, help them also to connect their work to those in other units and departments and to learn. In this way, the EdTech team is creating a space for learning and innovation to happen.

Conclusion and Future Directions

In "The Heart of Change," Kotter wrote that "People change what they do less because they are given analysis that shifts their thinking, than because they are shown a truth that influences their feelings" (2002, p. 1). He then described "See, Feel, Change" as the way individuals change, as opposed to "Analysis-Think-Change" (2002). Kotter argued that individuals need an emotional response to a situation in order to change their minds and behavior. Transmitting organizational culture through artifacts is a way to change and set organizational behavior by tapping into people's feelings.

In hindsight, EdTech campus leaders can look at the success of the office over the last decade and point to Innovation Celebrations and the Innovation Chase as contributing to that success, but actually assessing the efficacy of the office's initiatives in terms of creating change is a future plan for EdTech. The Hostos Online Learning Assessment (HOLA) task force (see Chap. 16) initially focused more on investigating student and faculty perceptions of online learning; however, assessing EdTech's initiatives is also part of their future plans.

What worked to create change and technology adoption over the last decade needs to be regularly evaluated for the future of EdTech at Hostos. As times change, technology and society change and as do the needs of students. The demographics of the South Bronx, and particularly of the students served by Hostos and their access to technology, change, and, therefore, the EdTech leaders need to be nimble and flexible. Over the years EdTech has generated continued energy for the Innovation Celebration by changing the format of the celebration. Switching the portion of time set aside for networking versus presentations or hands-on time with new technology means that attendees get to experience the celebration slightly differently each time.

Generally speaking, the Innovation Celebration seems, anecdotally, to have been successful in doing what Kotter described as necessary for change—feeling (2002). The badges, prizes, food, and feelings of excitement appealed to the participants' hearts. However, the future means looking to the Innovation Celebration, the Innovation Chase badges, and all the ways that EdTech transmits culture through artifacts, and continuing to be flexible and nimble, thereby meeting the changing EdTech needs of the Hostos community.

References

Daniels, J. (2013, February 5). MOOC to POOC: Moving from massive to participatory [web log comment]. Retrieved from https://justpublics365.commons.gc.cuny.edu/02/2013/mooc-to-pooc-moving-from-massive-to-participatory/

Ducoff, K. (2012, December 27). 5 tech companies set to impact higher education in 2013 [web log comment]. Retrieved from https://www.huffingtonpost.com/kevin-ducoff/higher-Education-tech_b_2278751.html

Higgins, J. M., & McAllaster, C. (2004). If you want strategic change, don't forget to change your cultural artifacts. *Journal of Change Management*, 4(1), 63–73. https://doi.org/10.1080/1469701032000154926 (Business Source Premier).

Hostos Community College, Office of Academic Affairs. (2013). Annual report, Office of Educational Technology, 2012–2013, 5.

Hostos Community College, Office of Academic Affairs. (2014). Annual report, Office of Educational Technology, 2013–2014, 6.

Hostos Community College Office of Educational Technology (HCC EdTech). (2018). *Innovations chase*. Retrieved from https://commons.hostos.cuny.edu/achievements/

Kotter, J. P. (2002). *The heart of change*. Boston: Harvard Business School Publishing.

Krehbiel, T. C., Salzarulo, P. A., Cosmah, M. L., Forren, J., Gannod, G., Havelka, D., et al. (2017). Agile manifesto for teaching and learning. *Journal of Effective Teaching*, 17(2), 90–111.

Mazoue, J. (2013, January 28). The MOOC model: Challenging traditional education. Retrieved from https://er.educause.edu/articles/2013/1/the-mooc-model-challenging-traditional-education

McNerney, J. (2006). Secrets of high-performing executive teams. *Vital Speeches of the Day*, 72(11), 349–352.

Meehan, P., Rigby, D., & Rogers, P. (2008). Creating and sustaining a winning culture. *Harvard Management Update*, 13(1), 3–5.

Senge, P. M. (2006). *The fifth discipline: The art and practice of the learning organization*. New York: Currency and Doubleday.

CHAPTER 10

Through the Eyes of an Early Adopter

Amy J. Ramson

This personal narrative written by an early adopter at Hostos describes the hurdles and promises of technology in the 1990s and early 2000s.

I have been teaching in the Criminal Justice and Paralegal programs at Hostos Community College since 1990. In the mid-1990s, as computers and cell phones were fast becoming part of our daily lives, I realized that it was essential for my students to become familiar with computer programs, databases, and the Internet. As young, entry-level employees in law and criminal justice, they would be expected to be computer savvy. I also recognized that I, myself, had to learn about instructional technology so that I could serve as a role model, teaching and inspiring my students. I enrolled in as many professional development classes as I could to learn about programs and the Internet. I remember that I was so unskilled that I had to take the beginner class twice—I did not even know how to use the mouse! I have also taken many courses to learn about developing online courses. One of the most helpful ones was a CUNY-wide online course, which put me in the shoes of a student.

In 1997, I joined the Committee on Computing (CAC) because I wanted to help move the college toward the goal of becoming a

---

A. J. Ramson (✉)
Behavioral and Social Sciences Department, Hostos Community College, CUNY, Bronx, NY, USA
e-mail: ARAMSON@hostos.cuny.edu

© The Author(s) 2019
K. S. Wolfe et al. (eds.), *Developing Educational Technology at an Urban Community College*, https://doi.org/10.1007/978-3-030-17038-7_10

technologically forward institution. I began teaching web-enhanced, face-to-face courses using a Blackboard website as supplementary, and I later developed hybrid and then asynchronous courses supported by professional development courses and mentors on the CAC. Many of the members of the CAC were senior and well-regarded faculty and they became my mentors and my friends. The chair and members of the committee were visionary and hardworking, and they built the strong foundation of instructional technology, which has been further enhanced by our current instructional technology staff.

One of the first projects we undertook was an assessment of the hardware, software, connectivity of the college, student access to technology, and the knowledge and interest in using technology of faculty and staff. The results indicated interest but demonstrated also that a lot of work was required. We found that many long-time faculty and even some students were unwilling to embrace computers and Blackboard. A constant hurdle has been resistance from supervisors who believe that online teaching requires less work than face-to-face instruction. Another hurdle that quickly dissipated was the lack of student access to computers at home and/or lack of quality home computers. In the late 1990s, we could not place a lot of media in an online course since some students could not access it on their computers.

The faculty and students have warmed to the use of technology little by little. In the early 2000s, students were still a bit unsure about how to navigate online courses. To date, I have noted a somewhat higher degree of acceptance of online instruction, which has probably also been aided by the integration of technology into every part of our lives.

Online learning has been beneficial for the retention of our population of students who possess financial and familial obstacles that prevent them from remaining in college. The majority of the students credit the flexibility of the online instruction and the accessibility of the materials, whether in PowerPoint and/or video, with their success. Examples of students who stand out for me include a mother of four who was pregnant with a fifth child and received an A grade in my rigorous hybrid course, and a day student last semester who was employed in an all-night job and was able to remain in my course because it was online.

I have judged that my students have greatly benefited from my use of technology in the classroom both from their anecdotal feedback and from my own assessment. Students review Panopto many times before an exam to better understand the material and are able to keep current with the class even if they miss an in-class session. I have noticed that the students are more interested in and can better understand certain subject matter when I bring in a digital form of instruction such as a video of a New York police-department COMPSTAT (short for comparative statistics) meeting or of a citizen's interaction with a police officer. Online classes help students develop the skills to work autonomously, and it provides them with confidence when they rely on their own initiative and succeed. At a community college where student support is woven into the fabric of our mission, there is a tendency or desire at times to spoon-feed the students. This overindulgence sets up the students for failure when they progress to a four-year college and/or begin to work. Students who have transferred to a four-year institution and visit us on campus have attributed part of their success to online courses. Online instruction is an ideal approach to teach students to work independently and also to teach them how to seek help when needed.

My class enrollment is consistently high even though I am a very demanding professor. In addition, we notice that there has been an increase in our paralegal enrollment and retention as a result of online classes because the students are employed and cannot attend face-to-face sessions. At present, I use Blackboard for all my courses; teach primarily in hybrid mode and fully online; record my lessons using Panopto; and telecommunicate using Collaborate Ultra, an essential tool in my fully online immigration law course.

My success in using instructional technology is fully attributable to the EdTech department and the CAC/ETLC committees (guided by the EdTech Director and Faculty Liaison) and the support provided by the EdTech personnel. When I joined the first iteration of the faculty committee, I was interested in utilizing instructional technology because of my curious nature and because I saw that it was essential for students pursuing criminal justice and law. However, I would have been unaware of the technological innovations were it not for the department and the committee who introduced me to every new innovation and has been a safe space in which I can experiment. I am certain that I would have not been able to use much of the technology had it not been for the EdTech personnel who consistently supported my efforts to use it. I know this because I regularly request extra help with Panopto and Collaborate Ultra. Through professional development classes, a mentorship program, my inspiring colleagues on the faculty committee, and the regular support provided by the EdTech personnel, I am now a mentor in this area.

When I reflect on my teaching career I can see that after ten years of teaching at Hostos, I was looking to enhance my teaching and my teaching experience. I was lucky to have found instructional technology and it has influenced and informed my career ever since. It has kept me passionate about teaching after 30 years and has been the focus of a lot of my scholarship in peer-reviewed journals and in presentations I have given domestically and abroad.

SECTION III

Opportunities and Challenges

CHAPTER 11

Preparing Our Students

George J. Rosa, David Dos Santos, and Carlos Guevara

Challenge Turned into Opportunity

Over the years, the Office of Educational Technology (EdTech) team heard the faculty voice concerns that students were not prepared for online learning. This chapter describes the Are You Ready? student online-learning readiness course, an effort to turn that challenge into an opportunity to better prepare students for online learning.

The team initially prepared students for online learning via online tutorials and in-person workshops. The team developed a "For Students" section on the website where students could access tutorials in various formats (video, text, etc.). The tutorials focused on Blackboard but also covered technology like clickers, iPads and other mobile devices, blogs and wikis, and lecture-capture and video-streaming applications. The tutorials were initially produced in-house but, in a move to increase consistency and uniformity, were eventually replaced by CUNY's set of online, downloadable print tutorials and Blackboard's own video tutorials on their YouTube

---

G. J. Rosa (✉) • D. Dos Santos
Hostos Community College, CUNY, Bronx, NY, USA
e-mail: grosa@hostos.cuny.edu; dsantos@hostos.cuny.edu

C. Guevara
Division of Academic Affairs, Hostos Community College, CUNY, Bronx, NY, USA
e-mail: cguevara@hostos.cuny.edu

© The Author(s) 2019
K. S. Wolfe et al. (eds.), *Developing Educational Technology at an Urban Community College*, https://doi.org/10.1007/978-3-030-17038-7_11

channel. EdTech staff also offered in-person workshops for students, which covered topics like Blackboard basics and the Microsoft Office suite. At first the Blackboard workshops were presented by the EdTech team to whole classes as requested by the instructor. The EdTech team then added open workshops that any students could attend. They registered through a home-grown registration application—and attended at their convenience.

There were challenges inherent in relying on tutorials and in-person workshops to improve students' readiness for online learning. The collection of tutorials was difficult and resource-intense to maintain and organize, and difficult for students and faculty to navigate. Communicating with faculty and students about which tutorials were most relevant for their courses and how to locate the tutorials was difficult, especially as both faculty and students tended to use their own personal email accounts rather than Hostos email. As there was no way to assess whether students completed the online tutorials, faculty members were often unsure that students had completed this work. The in-person workshops were difficult to schedule for students in fully online classes, and even in in-person courses, faculty often did not want to spend valuable class time teaching technology tools. Thus, the instructors of the online courses were left unsure of the degree of readiness of their students and expected a wide range of skills and competencies. The EdTech team understood these challenges and, in the fall of 2013, began work on the development of the Are You Ready? student online-learning readiness course that would be offered via Blackboard, the learning-management system (LMS) used by Hostos.

The team did considerable research before deciding to put resources into developing this course. The Hostos Office of Institutional Research compiled data for in-house use by the EdTech team about trends of students' success in online courses, which seemed to mirror results from national studies such as the annual student and technology reports from the Educause Center for Analysis and Research (ECAR), the Horizon Report from the New Media Consortium (now part of Educause), and Effectiveness of Online Learning from the Community College Research Center (CCRC) from Columbia University. From this research the team realized the need for students to become well-versed in the tools and strategies required for distance-learning success, understand time management, be comfortable with the multiple ways content is delivered to accommodate all users, learn to benefit from the learning communities and collaboration opportunities that can found online, and become familiar with the ethical considerations of working and socializing online.

When the EdTech team first began this endeavor, they explored methods used by other CUNY campuses for determining and encouraging students' readiness for online learning. Some campuses offered online surveys or suitability self-tests, intended for self-reflection and self-assessment by students on the reasons why they were considering going online with their studies, their attitudes about online as opposed to face-to-face learning, and whether they believed they possessed the skills, technical knowledge, discipline, and motivation for online learning. The intention seemed to be for students to make their own decisions on suitability based on their scores as well as the content of the questions. Most CUNY campuses offered workshops for students on Blackboard and other topics related to digital skills, such as Microsoft Office, as well as a directory for on-campus support. A few, such as Queensborough Community College, had a fairly comprehensive set of tutorials or modules posted on their website covering various topics of online learning, including what to expect in an online course, attributes a successful e-learner possesses, netiquette, academic integrity, technology requirements, new learning technologies, and campus services for students.

Additionally, Guevara chaired the Hispanic Educational Technology (HETS) Consortium Distance Learning Task Force from 2012 to 2014, whose charge was to explore how higher education institutions were preparing students and faculty for online learning. This task force developed a set of recommendations that were found to be fundamental in the preparation of students for the online environment, most of which were used in the creation of the Are You Ready? course.

The EdTech team was also concerned that faculty perceptions of students' readiness for online learning decreased faculty participation in the online learning initiative (see Chap. 5). The EdTech team frequently heard from the faculty that their students did not know Blackboard, and that students had difficulty with technology, or did not have access to technology. Some of the faculty believed that because many students were slightly older than traditionally aged students, they had less experience with computers and other digital devices. They also believed that the socio-economic status of Hostos students meant they would have less access to and less experience with technology (HCC OIRSA, 2016).

A lack of confidence in the digital skills students possess may be a common occurrence across campuses. According to the 2017 ECAR faculty and information technology survey, only about 50% of the faculty agreed or strongly agreed that their students are prepared to use institution-specific technology (Pomerantz & Brooks, 2017). Data from the same survey also showed that faculty were extremely reluctant (less than 10% for faculty) to ask their students for information about work-related technology, with nearly 75% putting their faith in campus help-desk services. Even "figuring out for themselves" was many times higher at about 60%, despite the fact that about 70% responded that faculty surveyed felt students were prepared to use basic software programs and applications. In his commentary in the *Journal of College Teaching,* David C. Dietrich of the University of Tennessee at Martin writes of his reluctance to transition to online instruction at Lambuth University. He lists many reasons for this, one of which was skepticism of the level of student digital competencies based on previous experience in instructing students lacking tech skills. He cites the high percentage of older students with job and family commitments, and felt that their requirement to learn Blackboard and other unfamiliar digital skills in addition to the regular coursework load would require additional time on their part. He also had to adjust his course content to include more information about Blackboard and other aspects of digital learning tools (2015).

Although there are studies such as those mentioned above that discuss student readiness as an obstacle for getting faculty buy-in for teaching online and hybrid courses, the data is not completely consistent. A desire to learn about Hostos student and faculty perceptions of online learning led the EdTech team to create the Hostos Online Learning Assessment (HOLA) Task Force (see Chap. 16). Some of the findings on the initial survey in 2015 suggested that faculty need not be concerned about students' readiness for online learning. In this survey, conducted among 198 students who were enrolled in online courses, 57% stated that the level of difficulty in an online course was the same as in an in-person course, with almost 20% agreeing that they were easier. By a large percentage—87.9%—students believed they had "adequate access to technology to complete the needs of the course." Survey data also indicated that students had little difficulty navigating to online courses and to syllabi, assignments and other content posted in the course sites (Wolfe et al., 2016). This survey was conducted every semester for the first two years and every year after that, producing consistent results regarding students' access to technology, which are similar to results found in recent national surveys about students access to technology such as the 2018 Educause report on students and technology, which indicated a high percentage of students that report having access to technology.

Another growing challenge was support of online learning by the help-desk operation. At Hostos there are three help desks that are available to students: the student technology help desk, the IT help desk that serves both students and faculty, and the EdTech team that, though mostly dedicated to support faculty in their use of technology in the classroom, also provided training to students in the use of classroom technologies supported by the college. Although the Hostos help-desk operations were able to address most technology issues that students face, there were still issues to resolve. As an increasing number of students enrolled in online courses, it was becoming a challenge for the help desks to keep up with demand. Additionally, as students in online courses accessed their courses 24/7, their questions came at every and any hour, yet it was difficult to fund and staff a 24/7 help desk. Finally, as a community college, expert peer tech-helpers (usually tech-savvy, part-time students) have potentially a relatively short career on campus before they move on to four-year colleges or full-time employment, requiring the constant training of new helpers.

In addition to offering the Are You Ready? course to ease students into online learning, the EdTech team worked to ensure that all Blackboard courses began each semester with a default structure created from a custom template, with areas for course content, syllabus, discussion, campus resources, video and web conferencing, and campus Blackboard support. The EdTech team believed that a consistent structure would help students navigate Blackboard courses more easily. This structure largely grew out of feedback from participants in the online initiative (see Chap. 7). Generally, the faculty follows this recommended course structure, but there are several members that modify it to conform to their own teaching styles and the particular course syllabus. Maintaining consistency in online course presentation across disciplines can alleviate some of the unnecessary complexities in the digital learning experience that distracts students from learning core academic content.

The EdTech team settled on this multi-pronged approach to encourage student success in the online environment—preparing them through the online readiness course, supporting them with the help desk, and continuing to offer workshops for those faculty who preferred in-person guidance for their classes. The EdTech team hoped that if students were better prepared for online learning, then online initiative would expand into disciplines whose faculty were hesitant to embrace online learning. As a result of this effort, faculty could decrease their skepticism toward online learning and focus on adapting and transitioning to online learning.

The Are You Ready? course was launched in spring 2014. The self-paced course was designed as a model online course that utilizes several Blackboard tools such as online quizzes and adaptive release, a feature that allows for control of the sequence and actions students have to take to access the content in the course. The course is divided into five distinct sections, and students start with a self-evaluation to assess personality and proficiency for taking an online course. Students learn about the technology, personal and educational habits, and etiquette for participation in the online environment (also known as netiquette). A badge and certificate are awarded on successful completion of the course to add an aspect of gamification and to provide students with a record that can be presented to their instructors. The course was designed to be completed in 30–60 minutes.

The Are You Ready? course is actively maintained by the EdTech team and is currently on its seventh revision. Are You Ready? starts with an introductory section followed by:

- Section 1: Welcome to CUNY Online Learning!
- Section 2: Basic Technology Proficiency
- Section 3: Using Blackboard
- Section 4: Technology Requirements
- Section 5: Netiquette

The course begins with a welcoming introduction, an explanation of hybrid and asynchronous online courses, and a suitability self-assessment test. It includes a page that guides students to the various campus support offices along with contact information, as well as an open discussion forum.

The course incorporates multimedia elements aimed at modeling universal design for learning (UDL) principles in Blackboard. UDL is a framework to improve and optimize teaching and learning for all people based on scientific insights into how humans learn (CAST Inc., 2018). Each section delivers content that addresses different learning styles by using mixed media such as video, images, text, and interactive elements. In order to track student interaction with the content and progress in the section, a feature in Blackboard called adaptive release is used, which allows a defined path of how and when students see the content. Generally, students are asked to click a "mark reviewed" button to continue and see the subsequent part of the section. Each section ends with a short assessment in which a score of 100% is required to move on to the next section, thus ensuring mastery of content. Students are permitted to retake an assessment an unlimited number of times, and in order to prevent skipping through the sections and gaming the course by guessing the answers of the assessment, question banks randomize the questions and answers in each quiz attempt. There are three to five possibilities for each question in a quiz.

Several technologies in addition to Blackboard were also incorporated to build the mixed-media content and accomplish a UDL approach. Video whiteboard software, free open-source audio-editing software, and entry-level equipment were used to create the different video components of the course. The course development and updating process of Are Your Ready? follows software development and instructional design methodologies such as AGILE and ADDIE to continuously revise and improve the content and user experience (UX) of the course, including accessibility. The course also includes a final satisfaction survey before students can claim their certificates of completion, which, in addition to serving as a tool to assess the student's experience with the course and their preparation for online learning, also serves to capture student comments on how the tool can be improved. The EdTech team also asked for comments from faculty who use Are You Ready? in their courses. The most common problems encountered or reported by students range from not being familiar with the sequential appearance of the content to not having read the instructions. In addition to improving the UX of the tool, EdTech now provides in-person guidance for Are You Ready? to those students who need it.

The elements covered in this course teach students to navigate the online environment, covering topics like understanding different systems and platforms, logon credentials, communication methods, and how online courses are structured. Despite the fact that this course is not mandatory for students who want to enroll in an online class, most faculty who teach online courses have included Are You Ready? as one of the first course assignments. A number of faculty who teach face-to-face but use Blackboard have also included Are You Ready? as an assignment. Anecdotally, the EdTech team has noted that faculty feedback is positive. Those who were once opposed to the idea of teaching online are starting to ask the team about online learning. Their curiosity is blossoming.

The EdTech team provides walk-in support for students who need one-to-one assistance with the Are You Ready? course. Initially the course required students to achieve a 70% pass rate on the module's quizzes and, after three attempts, required the students to visit the EdTech office to unlock the course. Students frequently, before going through the course, attempted to guess the quiz answers and were locked out. The EdTech team switched strategies and now the quizzes require 100% correct to pass, but students have unlimited attempts. After this change, the number of students visiting the EdTech office for help using the Are You Ready? course decreased dramatically. Anecdotally, faculty do not report that students need significant technology support to access and complete the Are You Ready? course.

Instructions to take the course appear on every hybrid and asynchronous course in the university's student-information system (CUNYFirst), and also on every course in Blackboard. The EdTech team has partnered with all of the colleges' advisement units so that advisors can suggest that students who are thinking of taking online courses complete the Are You Ready? course to determine if they are ready before deciding to register. Are You Ready? is also promoted on campus TV signage, flyers, email communications, college websites, and social media.

Preparing students for online learning is a challenge faced at many if not all of the CUNY campuses. Given that many Hostos students transfer to four-year colleges within CUNY, it made sense to join forces with other campuses and work on a common tool rather than multiple tools to solve the same problem. Breaking silos is challenging within an institution and even more challenging between institutions; however, after a successful pilot of the Are You Ready? course at Hostos, Guevara wanted to break these silos. He offered colleagues from the Bronx CUNY colleges, some of whom had already collaborated in the successful Bronx EdTech Showcase (see Chap. 3), the opportunity to try the course and join the team to further improve it. This invitation was also extended to other campuses across CUNY. The idea Guevara had in mind was to establish a consortium approach among the teams who wanted to adapt the course to (a) develop a common course across these colleges; (b) take advantage of the human resources from each college to utilize the multiple perspectives, skills, and expertise from these teams to continuously improve the course; (c) run cross-campus research projects to assess the effectiveness and further improve this course. The Are You Ready? course is currently being used by Bronx Community College, piloted by Lehman College and John Jay College, and explored by five other colleges.

The EdTech team received university-wide and national recognitions for the Are You Ready? course project. In 2016, the team received the CUNY Excellence in Technology Award during the 2016 CUNY IT conference. The CUNY IT conference is a yearly conference celebrating and exploring the use of technology in the classroom across all 24 CUNY campuses. In 2017, the EdTech team also received the Blackboard Catalyst award for Optimizing Student Experience; this award honors those institutions whose educational and administrative innovations have markedly improved the total learner experience (Blackboard Catalyst Awards, 2017). The Blackboard Catalyst Awards started in 2005 and recognizes innovation and excellence in the Blackboard global community of practice, where millions of educators and learners work every day to redefine what is possible when leveraging technology (Cohn, 2017).

As of fall 2017, the number of online courses offered at Hostos represented 9.1% of all course offerings, according to the 2017–2018 CUNY Performance Management Project (CUNY, 2018). This number includes approximately 100 online courses from about 1000 courses offered, which represents approximately 2000–2500 (non-unique) students enrolled in online courses every semester. With these numbers in perspective, there have been over 2700 who enrolled, about 2500 who took the self-assessment quiz, and about 1500 who completed the Are You Ready? course since it was deployed in fall 2014. Despite the fact that this course is not mandatory, the numbers are excellent.

This project exemplifies the Innovations Web and how the interconnectedness and dependence of each component is essential to guarantee the success of this project. Particularly, aligning support structures, providing timely support, establishing strong communication channels, building a community of support to increase student confidence about online learning and decrease skepticism among faculty, and identifying mechanisms for assessment and continuous improvement have contributed to the promotion of an organizational culture change as to how online learning is perceived and embraced at Hostos. The cycle of continuous improvement does not stop, and there are many areas for improvement and expansion in this project that have already started. For instance, the EdTech office has extended its hours of attention during the evenings and weekends, and also converted an instructional designer line to that of an online-learning coordinator to better support the expansion of online learning at Hostos. Also, the HOLA task force will research the experiences among advisors when working with students who are considering taking online courses and whether the use of the Are You Ready? course has been useful. Similarly, the EdTech team will continue to team up with the other colleges that adopted Are You Ready? to improve its content and UX, as well as to conduct cross-campus research about its impact and effectiveness. Future plans, with the support from the Office of Information Technology, also include the deployment of chatbot technology to extend and enhance the online support for students and faculty.

References

Blackboard Catalyst Awards. (2017). *Blackboard announces winners of 2017 Catalyst Awards*. Retrieved from http://press.blackboard.com/Blackboard-Catalyst-Awards-2017

CAST Inc. (2018, August 31). *About universal design for learning*. Retrieved from http://www.cast.org/our-work/about-udl.html#.XEHnZfxOlBx

Cohn, S. (2017, June 13). Blackboard announces winners of 2017 Catalyst Awards. *BlackBoard Newsroom*. Retrieved August 1, 2018, from http://press.blackboard.com/Blackboard-Catalyst-Awards-2017

CUNY. (2018). *Performance monitoring data book: 2017–2018 university report*. Retrieved from http://www2.cuny.edu/wp-content/uploads/sites/4/page-assets/about/administration/offices/oira/institutional/data/current-student-data-book-by-ubject/PMP_University_Data_Book_2018-Final_2018-08-16_v4.pdf

Dietrich, D. C. (2015). Observations of a reluctant online instructor: Transitioning from the classroom to the computer. *College Teaching, 63*(3), 93–98. https://doi.org/10.1080/87567555.2015.1019824.

Hostos Community College, Office of Institutional Research and Student Assessment (HCC OIRSA). (2016). *Student profile for spring 2016 term*. Retrieved from http://www.hostos.cuny.edu/Hostos/media/Office-of-the-President/Institutional-Research-Assessment/Profile-thru-S16.pdf

Pomerantz, J., & Brooks, D. (2017). *ECAR study of faculty and information technology*. Retrieved from https://www.educause.edu/ecar/research-publications/ecar-study-of-faculty-and-information-technology/2017/introduction-and-key-findings

Wolfe, K., Hoiland, S., Lyons, K., Guevara, C., Burrell, K. B., DiSanto, J. M., …, Ridley, L. L. (2016, April). Hostos online learning assessment: A survey of student perceptions. *Hispanic Educational Technology Services Journal, 6*. Retrieved from http://hets.org/ejournal/2016/04/28/hostos-online-learning-assessment-a-survey-of-student-perceptions/

CHAPTER 12

Expanding Access to Education Through Open Educational Resources (OERs)

Lisa Tappeiner, Jacqueline M. DiSanto, and Kate Lyons

Access to educational opportunities for traditionally underserved populations is core to the mission and history of Hostos Community College. It is not surprising that the Hostos faculty actively seek ways to keep the costs of education low for students while ensuring that they have access to educational programs that prepare them for majors at four-year colleges or for the workforce. For the past several years, Hostos has participated in a number of national and statewide initiatives designed to alleviate the cost of education by encouraging faculty to adopt open (low- or no-cost) alternatives to traditional, costly textbooks for classes and programs with high enrollment. Adapting a course to use only readings and supplementary materials that are free of copyright restrictions, and consequently either have no cost or are inexpensive for students to access, takes dedication and creativity on the part of the faculty; similar to creating an online course, this also involves a certain amount of risk.

L. Tappeiner (✉) • K. Lyons
Hostos Community College, CUNY, Bronx, NY, USA
e-mail: etappeiner@hostos.cuny.edu; clyons@hostos.cuny.edu

J. M. DiSanto
Education Department, Hostos Community College, CUNY, Bronx, NY, USA
e-mail: jdisanto@hostos.cuny.edu

© The Author(s) 2019
K. S. Wolfe et al. (eds.), *Developing Educational Technology at an Urban Community College*, https://doi.org/10.1007/978-3-030-17038-7_12

It is never easy to make changes in the way things have traditionally been done; this includes replacing traditional textbooks and supplementary study questions and quizzes with Open Educational Resources (OERs). However, developing and adopting OER materials aligns with a mission central to this institution—making education accessible to all students. This effort reflects the values that make Hostos Community College a unique place to teach and learn. This chapter discusses Hostos' OER initiatives and the broader implications of open access for community colleges and equity in higher education.

Background: OER and 5R Permissions

Open content describes any work that is either in the public domain or licensed in a way that makes it permissible for others to adapt and use content freely. In the early 2000s, educators were beginning to use digital technology to do what they had been doing in the analog world for decades: sharing the learning materials they had created and modifying materials that other educators had created for their own purposes. These materials became known as open-educational resources (OERs). The William and Flora Hewlett Foundation, longtime supporters of open education, defines OERs as "teaching, learning and research materials in any medium – digital or otherwise – that reside in the public domain or have been released under an open license that permits no-cost access, use, adaptation and redistribution by others with no or limited restrictions" (n.d.). At the same time, projects such as Creative Commons were developing a copyright framework for permitting the reuse of information and cultural content. Leading thinkers of open access identified five permissions granted to users of open content known as the 5 Rs:

1. Retain or make copies of content.
2. Reuse content, for example, in a lecture or a website.
3. Revise, for example, provide relevant examples for a specific context.
4. Remix or create something new using open content.
5. Redistribute or share copies with others (Wiley, 2016).

For community colleges, where students are likely to take survey courses that cover academic subjects broadly, OERs are typically created or adapted by faculty to replace textbooks, whose costs have been steadily increasing since the 1970s (Perry, 2012). Because OERs are often created and disseminated in digital formats, they easily incorporate sound, video, and animation in ways that extend beyond the traditional text-based format of textbooks. Online platforms, such as the OER Hub, bring together a growing body of research that documents the growth of the OER movement and its impact on community colleges in particular and higher education in general.

The Problem with Commercially Produced Textbooks

During the years that the EdTech team was gaining momentum—as a community of educators interested in offering support for colleagues who were seeking to experiment with new tools and methods for teaching—the campus community was beginning to grapple with a major challenge facing students of large-survey classes namely, the rising cost of textbooks. A 2015 report by a group of Student Public Interest Research Groups (student PIRGs) found that the cost of college textbooks had risen over 800% since 1978—more than three times the rate of inflation (Senack, 2014). Students who are assigned textbooks they cannot afford go without. They either spend precious study time making copies of required readings or skip the reading altogether. A 2014 study conducted by student PIRGs found that "65% of students had skipped buying or renting a textbook because it was too expensive and 94% of those students felt that doing so would hurt their grades in a course" (Senack, 2014). Similarly, a 2016 study conducted by researchers at Florida Virtual University found that skyrocketing textbook costs negatively affected a range of student success indicators. The high cost of textbooks contributed to students registering for fewer classes, dropping out of or withdrawing from courses for which they had registered, or failing courses outright. The survey found that although students in associate-degree programs are more likely to purchase textbooks than their counterparts in four-year colleges, almost half of all respondents reported that they have compensated for the high costs of textbooks either by taking fewer courses or by choosing their courses based on the price of the textbooks (Donaldson & Shen, 2016).

Although no survey of students has been conducted to formally quantify the situation at Hostos, faculty and librarians have been keenly aware for years that students frequently forgo purchasing costly required texts, even in core prerequisite courses such as Anatomy and Physiology and

Mathematics. In the academic year 2016–17, the average required textbook assigned at Hostos Community College cost more than $100, with the maximum price being $375. An analysis of Hostos Library acquisitions data shows that a full-time student enrolled in four to five classes per semester could expect to pay an average of close to $1000 for textbooks. The City University's 2016 Student Experience survey reports that over 70% of community college students live in households with incomes below $30,000 (CUNY, 2016). The number of low-income students at Hostos, located in one of the city's poorest congressional districts, is likely to be even higher. Clearly, the average cost of textbooks per semester is out of reach for most Hostos students, and it is a given that, for any survey course with high textbook costs, a significant number of students will make do without a personal copy.

Faced with the reality that many students show up to the class without the required textbooks, the faculty must be prepared to either accommodate these students or assign otherwise capable students lower grades because they do not have access to essential content. Often students opt to wait in long lines with others in the same predicament to make photocopies of needed textbook chapters borrowed from friends or checked out from the library's reserve collection, using valuable study time to get access to content rather than learning it. This unfortunate situation has only intensified over time as the cost of textbooks has risen dramatically, and it places one more obstacle in the path of an already vulnerable and stressed student population.

THE BEGINNINGS OF OER AT HOSTOS

The Executive Chief Librarian at Hostos, Professor Madeline Ford, approached the coordinator of the Early-Childhood Education (ECE) program, Dr. Jacqueline DiSanto, in spring 2016 about joining a consortium that was co-authoring an *Achieving the Dream* (AtD) grant application that would support the creation of completely OER-reliant programs by spring 2019. This initiative required the buy-in of a number of important parties who were initially unfamiliar with the concept of OERs, including five full-time ECE faculty members and the chairs of the academic departments that offered courses required within the ECE degree, such as English, Mathematics, and Psychology. The principal investigator of the grant was employed at the central office of The City University of New York (CUNY) and was submitting the application for a cohort of three community colleges within the university. The other two colleges were Borough of Manhattan Community College (for the Criminal Justice program) and Bronx Community College (for General Education with a History concentration). The grant was successfully funded for $300,000 to be shared among the three programs.

The first challenge was to build a team of OER experts on each campus capable of mentoring and supporting the development of programs. Faculty from the academic-content areas within ECE, who agreed to teach their courses using OERs, and librarians tasked with locating open materials and verifying their copyright status attended OER training. Several day-long workshops were designed to help attendees understand the purpose of the grant, appreciate the benefits of using textbooks and other educational resources whose content was free from copyright restrictions, and learn how to find and develop this content for their courses.

The idea behind the AtD grant was to develop entire degree programs with zero textbook costs. Typically, OER classes are scattered across a college's curricula and are often the work of an isolated faculty member committed to open education, but rarely are entire programs comprised of OER courses. As a result of the work done for this grant, community colleges around the country would have access to a range of OER content for the types of programs they commonly offer, such as Criminal Justice or Early-Childhood Education. The AtD grant also required the faculty to list each learning outcome for the course they were adapting and identify the OER that would help them meet each learning goal. In many cases, working on adapting a course to use OER materials provided an opportunity for the faculty to incorporate multimedia, primary sources, or other types of resources better suited than a textbook for meeting the objectives of the course. Finally, the grant required using only those materials with CC-BY Creative Commons licenses. This is the most open form of license, which allows others to share and make changes to work as long as credit is given to creators.

Becoming an OER Program

Although the AtD grant was focused on developing a fully OER Early Childhood Education program, it required the participation of colleagues from numerous content areas. The ECE program requires 20 courses spread across six academic departments (see Table 12.1), and the support of colleagues across the academic-content areas was needed to ensure that

Table 12.1 Early Childhood Education program-degree requirements

Department	Discipline	Courses (credits)
English	Composition & Literature	2 (6 credits)
Natural Sciences	Biology	2 (4 credits)
Mathematics	Mathematics	1 (3 credits)
Behavioral & Social Sciences	Psychology	1 (3 credits)
Behavioral & Social Sciences	History	1 (3 credits)
Education	Early-Childhood Education	9 (27 credits)
Education	Health Education	2 (6 credits)
Education	Physical Education	1 (1 credit)
Humanities	Modern Language	1 (3 credits)
Elective	Elective	1 (3 credits)

a student could enroll in the ECE program and complete all degree requirements by taking classes that use OERs in place of textbooks. It took many conversations to convince the necessary number of faculty and department chairs across the disciplines that this change would benefit students and enliven their own approach to teaching without sacrificing content and learning.

Faculty developers who agreed to be part of this project were instructed to focus on the course description that is included in the college catalog, the program or course-learning objectives, and all existing information in the syllabus. It was essential that the learning outcomes themselves did not change—just the resources used to meet them. As a result, no courses were revised nor did any need to be approved by college curriculum committees and the college-wide Senate. Developers listed learning outcomes for each course and then listed open resources that helped them meet these outcomes. Librarians and grant consultants would verify the copyright status of items in question and suggest alternate resources if an instructional resource was copyrighted or otherwise restricted. This was intended to be a change in resources—not in the course. The grant makers required only OERs that can be shared and revised by others to encourage the creation of completely open resources that can be adapted and adopted across institutions. The rigor and scope of the OERs needed to be equivalent to existing textbook content. Faculty OER course developers and librarians who assisted them all received stipends for their work.

Today, the Early-Childhood Education program—all 60 credits—is offered as a Zero Textbook Cost degree. In order to help students identify which course sections use OERs rather than traditional textbooks, the attribute ZERO Textbook Cost was created and is visible in a drop-down box and in the section information on their online enrollment system. This initial grant was followed by two others from the Gates Foundation and the State of New York, both of which also seek to support students moving through specific programs and target high textbook cost classes, such as Math and Science. As of fall semester 2018, Hostos offered more than 50 ZERO Textbook Cost sections across academic departments. The majority of these sections were developed or adapted using incentives from the OER grant initiatives.

An Opportunity to Build a Community of Pedagogical Developers

At Hostos, a college dedicated to providing access to both education and pedagogical innovation, open-education initiatives are about more than just saving the students' textbook money. They also provide an opportunity for faculty to investigate and develop new and hopefully more effective ways of delivering disciplinary content using media and digital tools as well as print sources. Faculty participating in OER course development are asked to connect each resource (a chapter in a textbook, a video, or an online simulation, etc.) to a course-learning objective. As a result, they are being asked to reflect on what they want their students to learn and how each resource helps students reach this goal.

As participants in the OER initiatives at Hostos, faculty can adopt an openly licensed resources as is, adapt materials from multiple OERs to put together a unique set suitable for their specific course, or create everything themselves. What does this look like? An individual or group of faculty might work together to create an educational resource that supports a specific learning objective. In this case, faculty might work with EdTech staff or librarians to license their newly created OER as CC-BY, which allows others to modify and reuse the content, and then share it on a number of OER platforms, including publishing it in Academic Works, CUNY's institutional repository. Faculty could also select passages of existing openly licensed material, including most government documents, most works published in the United States prior to 1923, and, most importantly, the growing number of open resources created by educators shared through a variety of OER or institutional repositories. Additionally, the grants described above allow the faculty to include supplemental materials that are not technically OERs but are freely available to users and may provide valuable content. TED Talks (which hold a more restrictive copyright license than resources with a CC license) and YouTube videos (subject to various copyright terms) are examples of this method available to faculty who might want to provide links to online sites that provide sound content.

For the first several years of the initiatives, librarians provided some support for the faculty adopting their courses to use OERs by locating and selecting resources available in online repositories with appropriate licenses. However, some faculty teach courses with content not sufficiently covered by existing OERs and may need the assistance of educational technologists to identify or create new content. Similar to their work in supporting online learning, EdTech has a pivotal role to play in training and supporting the faculty as they develop technology-driven OERs. For instance, the Office of Educational Technology (EdTech) licenses tools that help the faculty create online content—such as software for creating whiteboard videos, lecture-captured presentations, and graphic-design programs. Support and training for these tools help the faculty participating in online initiatives and can also serve those faculty developing OER content. Moreover, EdTech is in a unique position to educate online-course developers about licensing their own teaching materials openly and raising awareness about ways of finding the excellent open resources already in existence. The EdTech team is also considering ways to use EdTech's Innovation Chase and Innovation Celebration to bolster the network of OER developers.

It is also important to note that not all subjects lend themselves to using OERs. For instance, twentieth and twenty-first century Literature courses primarily focus on texts that are covered by copyright. The same is true for Film Studies. Even in History classes, students may be asked to read primary sources that exist in the public domain, but many copyrighted textbooks and learning resources add contextual information or reformat texts or images to make them more readable. In the end, the goal should be to determine where OERs fit best in the curriculum and support their use and creation.

VALUING THE WORK OF COMMUNITY COLLEGE FACULTY

As part of The City University of New York (CUNY), a public institution in the country's largest city, Hostos Community College is devoted to educating a diverse student population, many of whom face significant educational and economic challenges as they enter their first years of college. Faculty at CUNY's community colleges teach a heavy course load, work with students with significant developmental needs, and are expected to maintain a substantial research agenda to be considered for tenure and promotion. Curriculum development of any kind rarely receives consideration equal to research and scholarship in terms of reappointment, tenure, and promotion decisions, in part because the work of teaching is difficult to capture and quantify (see Chap. 13). However, CUNY's institutional repository, Academic Works, provides a platform for OER developers to publish their work. Moreover, Academic Works is indexed by Google, which makes OERs findable by educators around the world, and it tracks the numbers of views and downloads. Although imperfect, the ability to publish and share educational and curricular materials through the institutional repository helps faculty make the case that, like more traditional forms of scholarship, not only curricular materials can be shared among colleagues in their departments, but they have the potential to support and inform the work of educators across the world. Academic Works supports community college faculty by providing a platform to publish and share the excellent open resources they have created within their disciplines and, hopefully, to improve the status of the difficult work of teaching and curricular development across the academic community.

In addition to giving faculty the opportunity to share their OERs, like other forms of scholarly communication, Academic Works gives faculty a vehicle through which they receive feedback about their content. Faculty and administrators at other campuses can contact faculty whose works are uploaded to Academic Works. In creating this platform and community for reflecting on and gaining feedback about OERs, faculty also find themselves in an environment that promotes research about the effectiveness of their educational and curricular materials and could potentially encourage and further scholarship in teaching and learning.

OERs Support Equality in Higher Education

Hostos Community College was founded half a century ago with the mission of providing access to higher education in the largely Spanish-speaking and immigrant community of the South Bronx. Over the years, the economic barriers that make earning a college degree extremely challenging for Hostos students have persisted—from lack of affordable childcare and decent housing to having to choose between buying food or textbooks. Building an initiative to integrate OERs into the culture of curriculum development at this college is, at its core, a way to address the economic pressures the students face daily. However, developing free or low-cost OERs is only a drop in the bucket. Much larger shifts in the ways wealth and resources are allocated in this society are needed to truly help students overcome the many challenges that make it difficult to complete a college degree and to make a successful transition to a four-year college or the workforce.

It is not surprising that Hostos is part of a significant and growing movement that views creating and using open educational resources in higher education as a practical way to address inequality in America's higher-education system. Open-education advocate Robyn DeRosa considers the potential of open access to change the values and practices of higher education:

> My blossoming hope is that we can use some of the tools and rhetoric of open to build a public response to the crisis in American public higher education . . . Open-access publishing can help our public institutions share research and information with the public, which would then set a logical premise for restoring state allocations and federal funding. Open pedagogies that empower learners to contribute to the shape of knowledge can assure that the labor markets they graduate into are responsive to their vision for the future of our societies. (2017)

Engaging in OER initiatives on this campus has not only reinvigorated conversations about the materials we use to teach, but it has also sparked discussions about our values as academics, the purpose of reading, and what it means to be a college that proudly sees itself as a rare catalyst for social mobility in an increasingly unequal society.

OERs: Looking Ahead

After almost three years of intensive work and multiple grants, the OER initiative at Hostos has a solid foundation. For the most part, faculty who have integrated OERs into their course design have no intention of returning to their former commercial textbooks. This suggests both a reasonable level of satisfaction with the initiative and a dedication to the value of open pedagogies. The challenge looking ahead is less about convincing faculty that OERs are good for students and more about ensuring that they will have the support needed, not only to expand OER offerings but also to update existing OERs for currency and accuracy. Just like commercial textbooks, OERs need to be continually revisited to reflect on emerging trends and new knowledge in their disciplines.

Beyond ensuring that faculty receive ongoing support to update OERs, next steps for the initiative should focus on ways to lower the cost of materials for the most students possible. The OER initiative should target courses with either high textbook costs or high enrollments. Also, given that most OERs are online, it makes sense to target online courses. Faculty who teach online are already using a learning-management system (LMS) to deliver content to students who are savvy about how to access content online. Although they require students to purchase commercially produced e-books to accompany their courses, thereby keeping the content digital, there is enough open-access digital content, which integrates well with Blackboard, to meet the needs of many courses with already-existing open resources. Another significant challenge would be to determine the best way to host OER content, both text and multimedia, and to ensure that it is easily accessible over time to the college community and beyond.

OERs are here to stay. It is up to the educators at Hostos and across all higher-education institutions to create and revise open educational resources that reflect high academic standards, make effective use of technology, and are easily accessible to our students and college students across the country. This mission has engaged and energized a significant segment of our academic community, and we are proud to be part of a movement that eases the financial burden of higher education for thousands of students.

References

City University of New York Office of Institutional Research and Assessment. (2016). *CUNY student experience survey 2016.* Retrieved from http://www2.cuny.edu/wp-content/uploads/sites/4/page-assets/about/administration/offices/oira/institutional/surveys/2016_SES_Highlights_Updated_10112016.pdf

DeRosa, R. (2017, November 1). OER: Bigger than affordability. *Inside Higher Ed.* Retrieved from https://www.insidehighered.com/digital-learning/views/2017/11/01/oer-catalyst-nationalconversation-about-public-higher-education

Donaldson, R. L., & Shen, E. (2016). *2016 Florida student textbook & course materials survey.* Tallahassee, FL: Florida Virtual Campus. Retrieved from https://oerknowledgecloud.org/sites/oerknowledgecloud.org/files/2016%20Student%20Textbook%20Survey.pdf

Institute of Educational Technology. The Open University *Open Education Research Hub.* Retrieved from http://oerhub.net/

Perry, M. J. (2012). The college textbook bubble and how the "open educational resources" movement is going up against the textbook cartel. *Carpe Diem/American Enterprise Institute.* Retrieved from http://www.aei.org/publication/the-college-textbook-bubble-and-how-the-open-educational-resources-movement-is-going-up-against-the-textbook-cartel/

Senack, E. (2014). *Open textbooks: The billion dollar solution.* Washington, DC: Center for Public Interest Research. Retrieved from https://studentpirgs.org/reports/sp/open-textbooks-billion-dollar-solution

Wiley, D. (n.d.). *Defining the "open" in open content and open educational resources.* Retrieved from http://opencontent.org/definition/

William and Flora Hewlett Foundation. (2019). *Open education resources.* Retrieved from https://hewlett.org/strategy/open-educational-resources/

CHAPTER 13

Creating a Safe Environment for Innovators

Lisa Tappeiner, Kate Lyons, Sandy Figueroa, and Linda Ridley

The Office of Educational Technology plays a central role in the Hostos Community College academic community by providing resources and services that support faculty and other educators as they explore and adopt new ways of teaching and conducting scholarship using emerging educational technologies. This essential role involves providing training, support, and resources for faculty, staff, and students, as well as being vocal advocates—of the benefits of technology for teaching and research—to key decision-makers on campus.

A main concern for many new faculty is how their use of educational technology will impact their path to tenure and promotion. Because their continued employment and promotion is recommended by their departmental peers and chair, faculty are motivated to take on initiatives approved by their colleagues. Ultimately, decisions for tenure and promotion are made by the provost and president; however, recommendations from the committees that evaluate faculty for tenure and promotion influence in these decisions. Thus, for new faculty, it is important to do work that their

---

L. Tappeiner (✉) • K. Lyons
Hostos Community College, CUNY, Bronx, NY, USA
e-mail: etappeiner@hostos.cuny.edu; clyons@hostos.cuny.edu

S. Figueroa • L. Ridley
Business Department, Hostos Community College, CUNY, Bronx, NY, USA
e-mail: sfigueroa@hostos.cuny.edu; lridley@hostos.cuny.edu

© The Author(s) 2019
K. S. Wolfe et al. (eds.), *Developing Educational Technology at an Urban Community College*, https://doi.org/10.1007/978-3-030-17038-7_13

colleagues and the college's administration understand and value. Faculty are evaluated on the basis of their teaching successes and efforts, their contribution to the scholarship in their fields, and their service to the college community. Encouraging tenured faculty, especially department chairs, to value curriculum development that incorporates educational technology and online learning is critical for supporting technology-minded faculty through the tenure and promotion process.

This chapter will describe how the EdTech team works to establish a supportive environment for exploration and innovation by ensuring that the committees and administrators who make decisions regarding tenure and promotion value pedagogical excellence in all modalities, including online teaching. This chapter will also discuss how EdTech advocates for and seeks to promote understanding of evolving digital forms of scholarship, such as digital humanities, so that they are valued equally to traditional forms of scholarship, such as peer-reviewed journal articles, by governance bodies that make decisions about appointments, tenure, and promotion.

Guidelines for Reappointment, Promotion, and Tenure: An Opportunity to Support Faculty

Like many academic institutions, Hostos Community College is governed by a complex set of rules and traditions that govern appointment, reappointment, tenure, and promotion. Hostos Community College is governed by the agreement between the Professional Staff Congress (PSC) and the City University of New York (CUNY) as well as the Board of Trustees Bylaws, and the Hostos Charter of Governance. These documents ensure high academic standards and consistency in decisions regarding appointment, reappointment, tenure, and promotion. Although some governance policies and practices are specific to Hostos, many are shared by all 24 campuses of the City University of New York (CUNY). Moreover, these documents are meant to protect the individual faculty member and the college while still upholding academic freedom and encouraging creativity. As technology changes academic practices, in both teaching and scholarship, the systems in place for reappointment, tenure, and promotion, as well as the organizational culture, need to be flexible enough to fairly evaluate faculty whose teaching practices, service, and scholarship have adopted new technology that are not explicitly addressed in current guidelines.

The PSC is the union that represents all university employees, and its purpose is "to advance and secure the professional and economic interests of the instructional staff of the City University and other members of the bargaining units of the Professional Staff Congress, with special regard for the interest of students and the City University" (PSC CUNY, 2015).

In the early 2000s, in an attempt to make concrete the specific expectations of faculty members as they progress through the process of appointment, reappointment, tenure, and promotion, each department created a set of guidelines to augment the general language of the legal documents that bind the college and the faculty member and assist department chairs and mentors in guiding untenured faculty. Personnel and Budget (P&B) committees at both the departmental and the college-wide levels have an ongoing charge to review the guidelines to ensure they consistently reflect departmental academic standards and, ideally, incorporate evolving forms of scholarship and artistic production. Consequently, P&B committee members are expected to be acquainted with reputable scholarly discourse within their fields and knowledgeable about potential venues for publication.

In addition to the guidelines described above, portfolios were introduced at Hostos in the early 2000s as a way for faculty to highlight their achievements as well as provide an opportunity for them to share their philosophy of education, teaching strategies, and their growth as professionals in their field. Newly appointed faculty are required to create portfolios that record their reflections and document their progress in scholarship, service, and teaching. They update these portfolios annually in the seven years prior to tenure for review by the departmental and college-wide P&B committees. Similar portfolios are used as a basis for consideration for promotion. Faculty portfolios serve as an important vehicle for new members of the college community to document growth as scholars and teachers.

The portfolio is a particularly effective tool for practitioners of digital and non-traditional forms of scholarship and teaching to explain in their own words the value of their work and to provide visual examples when appropriate. Prior to the introduction of portfolios, faculty submitted materials for reappointment and tenure without the opportunity to explain the significance of their work or to reflect upon their growth. In such a situation, they were at the mercy of their department chairs to understand, value, and advocate for their accomplishments in teaching and scholarship when presenting candidates to the college-wide P&B committee.

The content of the portfolios reflects how the faculty meet certain benchmarks outlined in the guidelines for tenure and promotion as they progress through their pre-tenure careers. Guidelines are published on the college's website and are visible to the campus community. Departmental P&B committees are responsible for ensuring that they are regularly updated to reflect current best practices and departmental expectations in teaching and research in each discipline. This process of revision presents an opportunity for the EdTech Leadership Council (ETLC), which comprises faculty representatives from each academic department (see Chap. 8), to advocate for including technology-enhanced teaching and scholarship as work that will advance a new faculty member toward tenure. Providing language to departmental committees charged with updating and revising their guidelines to include activities related to online teaching and scholarship is a significant example of how the EdTech team is working to support new modes of scholarship and teaching. At Hostos, it has supported new faculty who engaged in developing an online section of a heavily subscribed English course or curating a digital-animation festival and ensured that these endeavors were fully appreciated by committees that make decisions on reappointment, tenure, and promotion.

Rethinking the Teaching Observations for Online Contexts

Each semester, tenure-track faculty are required by contract to receive a teaching observation and participate in a follow-up conference as part of their annual evaluation. Typically, pre-tenure faculty are observed in their classrooms by more experienced colleagues within their departments. However, for years, the college lacked adequately prepared faculty to conduct observations in the online setting. This situation placed online instructors and departments in an uncertain position because online instructors did not receive potentially supportive and helpful feedback on what they were doing in their online-teaching environments nor were they establishing a formal record of teaching excellence in that online venue. Several years ago, a committee comprising faculty and academic administrators, including the former director of EdTech Dr. Loreto Porte was formed to develop formal guidelines and procedures for conducting collegial observations in online courses in an effort to provide relevance to the observation form for the online-learning practitioners. The goal was to ensure that observations in online classes are conducted with consistent diligence and quality across departments and that results are communicated to faculty being observed.

The Peer Observation Improvement Network for Teaching (POINT) was established in 2011 by the Office of Academic Affairs to research and disseminate best practices in conducting collegial classroom observations. Until Carlos Guevara joined the committee in 2014, there was no representation from EdTech, despite the fact that observations were being conducted in both asynchronous and the online portions of hybrid courses. The committee has since established guidelines for evaluating the learning environment for courses taught in hybrid course sections. These guidelines were based in part on guidelines for conducting peer observations in completely online classes, which predated the formation of POINT.

Observers of online instruction are asked to evaluate not only how the content is delivered but also how well the instructor employs tools specific to online teaching to facilitate student learning. For example, evaluators are encouraged to assess the effectiveness of methods used to facilitate communication between students and instructor as well as among students, such as discussion boards. Applying rigor and consistency in evaluating teaching regardless of teaching modality is best practice. The purpose of these guidelines to observe online courses was to help ensure that online teaching receives the same consideration and attention as traditional classroom instruction.

Although the guidelines were in place, they were rarely used because observation in the classroom was done using the same form for face-to-face courses, a form that was last revised in 1999. Another challenge when observing a class in the online environment is how to make it comparable to observing a timed, face-to-face period and not go beyond the equivalent class lesson in the learning-management system. The POINT committee embarked on a long journey in an effort to address these problems and based its recommendations on research and best practices to update the current peer-observation form. The objective of the committee was not only to incorporate all teaching modalities in one form, but also to provide more guidance and emphasize the importance of seeing the peer-observation process as an opportunity to improve teaching and professional growth. The committee also included in its plans the creation of adequate professional development to contribute to a change in the culture of peer observation at Hostos.

In fall 2018, a revised peer-observation form was approved by the college's Instructional Evaluation committee and the college-wide Senate and is to be implemented across the college in fall 2019. This new document includes specific indications for online observations that will eliminate the need for separate guidelines and emphasizes the importance of framing observation within equivalent limitations, such as when looking at a face-to-face class.

Subjectivity and the Tenure and Promotion Process

While the written, established guidelines for evaluating faculty for tenure and promotion should make the process objective, the reality is that P & B committee members bring their own perceptions of their colleagues to the table. Ultimately, although measures have been taken to make this process fair and transparent, it is an inherently conservative process by which faculty are appointed, re-appointed, and granted tenure, and, as such, they may constitute an institutional barrier to using new technology-driven approaches to teaching and scholarship, particularly by less self-confident or new-to-teaching faculty.

All members of P & B committees are tenured faculty, many of whom received their degrees decades ago and may be less likely to be engaged in digital scholarship and online teaching than more recently hired colleagues, who are introduced to EdTech initiatives through their new-faculty orientation. Pedagogical effectiveness is particularly difficult to evaluate, and the evaluation of online teaching, either partially or fully online, may be particularly challenging for faculty accustomed to teaching face-to-face. For example, instructional design, the effective use of recording and conferencing software, and providing timely feedback to online students are not readily apparent through traditional modes of teaching assessment. As any faculty member who is truly committed to online teaching can attest, there is a great deal of training and preparation that goes into an effective online course, which is difficult if not impossible to showcase in a printed faculty portfolio. The creation of guidelines for observers of online classes described above helps make the criteria for successful online teaching more transparent. However, there is more work to be done to ensure that the promotion process recognizes the effort involved in teaching in this modality by the faculty, especially pre-tenure faculty who are deeply committed to teaching online.

New faculty at Hostos are evaluated on the basis of teaching, scholarship, and service, but even at a community college with a heavy course load and many students in need of extra academic support, scholarship is the activity that is most easily measured and most highly valued in decisions regarding reappointment, tenure, and promotion. The culture of the college has yet to be fully cognizant of the breadth and depth of work involved in improving pedagogy by exploring, sharing, and creating new and innovative approaches to teaching. This is true of online learning but also of other non-traditional modalities such as service and team-based learning. Centering the work of pedagogical development and risk-taking is difficult. However, it is absolutely vital to students who will be working in increasingly team-centered, technology-rich environments, and to faculty who work to support them through pedagogical modalities that help them succeed beyond college.

At Hostos, the administration has been supportive of faculty who wish to move their courses to the online environment, and university-wide, broadening online course and program offerings is encouraged. However, sometimes department chairs only reluctantly authorize courses to be taught online for a number of reasons that can include being short of faculty to cover other courses; this can result in the online offerings being dropped after a few semesters. Untenured faculty have little recourse but to acquiesce to the needs of the department, and, if departmental leadership cannot support the online initiative, faculty will not have the opportunity to teach the courses they developed. In some cases, the reverse is true: The department chair may be enthusiastic about offering a course online, and faculty may be reluctant to make the change. In either case, enthusiasm for teaching online as well as the ability to actually schedule online courses varies widely from department to department and is often unpredictable. The same applies to other non-traditional teaching modalities, such as service and team-based learning.

The EdTech team and the college's Center for Teaching and Learning are strong forces in advocating at the departmental and collegial levels by providing professional development and recognizing pedagogical innovation on campus to ensure that faculty who do the hard work of trying new approaches and deepening their pedagogical practice are duly supported for their efforts. These efforts are paying off and have helped the college to continue to increase the number of online course offerings (see Chap. 7).

The Changing Face of Scholarship and Academic Publishing

The format of all types of scholarships across the disciplines is evolving, and the need to develop methods of evaluation that value the full range of scholarship, including digital scholarship, will only become more crucial with time. In a lecture on digital scholarship, Clifford Lynch and Don Carleton (2012) described emerging forms of scholarship: "We're also seeing the production of scholarly works that go far, far beyond traditional articles and traditional printed monographs—works that represent databases, that represent simulations, that represent complex mixtures of software and data analysis" (p. 463). He went on to emphasize that these multifaceted works are created, not just in fields like science and engineering, but also in the social sciences and the humanities. Faculty teaching digital animation and music may find themselves on the cutting edge of digital scholarship today, but it is only a matter of time before all academic departments will be confronted with the need to be able to appreciate and critically evaluate digital scholarship in their fields.

In addition to the acceptance of digital scholarship, the members of EdTech and ETLC faculty monitor venues for scholarly exchange and communication that do not necessarily conform to traditional forms of peer-reviewed scholarship. Empirical studies on the traditional peer-review process, a practice that has gone largely unchanged since the eighteenth century, show that it is far from perfect and may suffer from reviewer bias and/or lack of knowledge or expertise on a subject (Birukou et al., 2011). Researchers at the Center for Studies in Higher Education identified the need for a "reexamination of the locus, mechanisms, timing, and meaning of peer review" to be among the top concerns of faculty scholars (Hartley, Acord, Earl-Novell, Lawrence, & King, 2010). Alternatives to traditional forms of peer review, particularly in the sciences, include paper-ranking, bidding to review a piece, and using surveys of experts to evaluate quality (Birukou et al., 2011). The future of experiments in academic quality-control remains uncertain, and traditional peer review is still the accepted norm, but it is important to keep an eye on emerging trends and ensure that the committees and processes that make crucial decisions about the future of untenured faculty are aware of current trends in scholarly communication and review.

Another development that has had a significant impact on scholarly publication and communication is open access. Traditional publishers are experimenting with alternative models to paid subscriptions, such as author fees, and non-traditional publishers, such as libraries, are launching their own open-access publishing platforms. Although open access has the potential to expand opportunities for scholars to publish and disseminate their work, it can also cause confusion among academics charged with evaluating the quality and impact of open-access publications. The EdTech team sees its role as understanding these developments in academic publishing, made possible largely as a result of collaborative technology and educating the college community about the advantages and challenges of open-access publishing.

Institutional repositories present an opportunity for the EdTech team to continue to educate the community about alternatives to traditional academic-publishing venues, such as peer-reviewed journals, and to advocate for the value of scholarly output that does not fit neatly into the traditional container of a peer-reviewed article. Many colleges and universities provide repositories that make freely available academic and creative works by faculty, administrators, and students. Hostos is part of CUNY's institutional repository, Academic Works, which hosts almost 20,000 papers in 1031 disciplines (n.d.). Not only do institutional repositories provide a stable, open-access archive of the academic output of an institution, but they also allow for the broader dissemination of academic, educational, or artistic resources in all formats that have until recently been difficult to locate and have not received full consideration as important contributions to academic or cultural conversations. These formats include datasets, animations, recorded lectures, podcasts, white papers, learning objects, and student research. Academic Works presents a vital outreach opportunity for Hostos, a community college with a heavy faculty teaching-load, serving non-traditional students from a variety of linguistic and ethnic backgrounds. It enables the faculty to publish and disseminate the products of their work as educators and scholars that may not result in a peer-reviewed article, but are nevertheless significant contributions to knowledge and culture, from animations and games in the Digital Design program to research with students related to nutrition in the South Bronx Latino community.

Increasing awareness of Academic Works among faculty and administrators supports a more inclusive view of scholarship and teaching across campus. The EdTech team has worked on outreach programs to encourage and train faculty to upload their scholarly work and educational artifacts to the repository. At events organized by EdTech such as the Bronx

EdTech Showcase (see Chap. 6), participants are encouraged to upload slides and handouts from their presentations to the repository. Contributors receive reports from the system on how often their work is accessed by scholars around the world and a sense of the impact of their work. As the repository continues to be seeded by projects, publications, and educational artifacts, awareness of its impact and new ideas for ways to contribute increase over time.

ePortfolios: An Opportunity for New Scholarship

The physical format of the portfolio that the faculty are required to submit to be considered for reappointment, tenure, and promotion is a three-ring binder. This paper format works well to house and display traditional forms of scholarship and publications, such as chapters or articles, and printouts of slides from conference presentations. However, for faculty in newly established programs such as Digital Design and Music, whose artistic and creative work and teaching artifacts often exist primarily in a digital format, this paper-based format makes it difficult to fully display and communicate the scope of their work. The same has always been true for faculty in the visual and performing arts program, whose professional work is often difficult to capture and display in a print portfolio.

The faculty and staff involved with the EdTech Office have a crucial role to play as advocates for acceptance of emerging forms of digital scholarship across the disciplines. One opportunity that the EdTech team has researched is the ePortfolio for faculty. The EdTech staff selected a vendor, Digication, to host ePortfolios at Hostos, primarily for students. However, as faculty began learning the technology for use in their classes, they also began to experiment with showcasing their own work on ePortfolios. At this point, some faculty members have created their own ePortfolios, but they currently augment—not replace—the three-ring binder portfolio format. See Chap. 6 to learn about the benefits of ePortfolios from the student and academic perspectives.

The EdTech team has had conversations with administration, some department chairs, as well as some members of the college-wide P&B committee about the possibility of switching to ePortfolios. At this moment, there are still challenges. Because digital work is so easy to update, there are concerns about the editing process for ePortfolios. A timeline for updating binders would be crucial to ensure that all members of P&B committees evaluate the same version of each faculty member's ePortfolio. Additionally, ensuring access to the ePortfolios, while maintaining the privacy of faculty members, is challenging. As technology evolves, challenges like these become less insurmountable, but the challenge of changing organizational culture, as well as training all faculty on using the ePortfolio content-management system, remains. The EdTech team has begun looking to ePortfolios but is still in the early stages of encouraging the campus to adopt them for the faculty members' tenure and promotion process.

Power in Organizational Culture and Politics

The EdTech office seeks to be a voice for all faculty who take the time to explore and apply new teaching and learning modalities by providing technological support and resources and college-wide advocacy. They are mindful that, in addition to the power structures embedded in the hierarchy of Hostos' organizational culture and the power wielded by the P & B committees, other more traditional power differentials are also likely to exist at the college. Power differentials often found in higher education, such as the perceived higher ranking of some disciplines, as well as race and minority status, gender, and sexual orientation, can be found at Hostos as they are in all institutions of higher education.

Eddy and Ward (2015), for example, described how "women in community colleges were disproportionately represented in middle-level ranks" and outlined the consequence: "Middle-level leadership positions can actually slow advancement if too much time and attention is paid to management versus leadership and teaching versus administration. Mid-level managers may keep the trains running on time, but they do not get to choose the destination of the train" (p. 9). Being actively engaged with the initiatives in the EdTech Office is an opportunity to practice and develop leadership and management skills. Faculty, especially the new ones, might not find opportunities in their departments for leadership, as some positions are only open to tenured faculty, and others are simply already occupied. The EdTech Office, however, has many positions on committees and initiatives, many of which are highly regarded and award-winning within CUNY and externally. The EdTech team has always tried to be supportive of faculty who want to pitch and lead new ideas. The team tries to be cognizant of the need to help faculty take risks and practice their leadership.

The ongoing question remains for the EdTech team: How can we initiate an environment that not only encourages the integration of technology into teaching but also fully recognizes the challenges overcome in order to integrate technology into pedagogy? What behaviors can be maximized to enhance the practice of online pedagogy, both in delivery and in learning? At least a partial answer to this question may be found in the work of noted change management theorist Edgar Schein:

> …all forms of learning and change start with some form of dissatisfaction or frustration generated by data that disconfirm our expectations or hopes… Disconfirming information is not enough, however, because we can ignore the information, dismiss it as irrelevant, blame the undesired outcome on others or fate, or, as is most common, simply deny its validity. To become motivated to change, we must accept the information and connect it to something we care about. The disconfirmation must arouse what we can call "survival anxiety," or the feeling that if we do not change, we will fail to meet our needs or fail to achieve some goals or ideals that we have set for ourselves. (1999, 60)

Hostos Community College is certainly not alone in trying to meet the challenges of online pedagogy. This chapter has examined how faculty going through the process of reappointment and tenure are advised to forego any electronic-portfolio records in favor of hard-copy documentation. This limitation alone is enough to discourage the faculty from incorporating technology into their teaching and scholarship. Through its educational initiatives and efforts, the EdTech team seeks to cultivate an understanding of the change methodology throughout the campus to successfully integrate online teaching and scholarship into a long-standing campus culture that predates the large-scale integration of technology in our culture.

Change methodology must be carefully introduced to address areas of resistance among faculty, administrators, and students. Organizations draw on multiple resources in order to affect change (Bloodgood & Salisbury, 2001). One management technique to affect change is outlined by Kurt Lewin's change theory. Lewin, a twentieth-century organizational psychologist, fostered a three-stage model of change: (a) *Unfreezing*, by creating the right environment for risk-taking and innovation; (b) *changing* by providing support during the transformation; (c) *refreezing* by anchoring and reinforcing change (Kinicki & Fugate, 2018). EdTech plays a significant role in all three stages of this model. As we take a step back to examine the important work of our technology innovators at Hostos Community College, we have to acknowledge that true success requires resources in all three stages.

Hostos Community College's technology innovators have the potential for wider recognition among students seeking technology-rich experiences, especially with our award-winning focus on digital-learning technologies. The friction naturally occurs when there is a breakdown in the flow of effort from those faculty who might want to learn how to deliver a digital curriculum and, for instance, might not be able to see the fruition of their work in action due to scheduling constraints. In order to thrive as an educational institution, faculty should feel intrinsically motivated to learn and develop as educators. For the EdTech team to support transformation, it is crucial that the desire to develop as educators does not misalign with the survival anxiety that faculty feel when they think about the process of tenure and promotion.

REFERENCES

Birukou, A., Wakeling, J., Bartolini, C., Casati, F., Marchese, M., Mirylenka, K., et al. (2011). Alternatives to peer review: Novel approaches for research evaluation. *Frontiers in Computational Neuroscience, 5*(5). https://doi.org/10.3389/fncom.2011.00056.

Bloodgood, J. M., & Salisbury, W. D. (2001). Understanding the influence of organizational change strategies on information technology and knowledge management strategies. *Decision Support Systems, 31*, 55–69.

Eddy, P. L., & Ward, K. (2015). Lean in or opt out: Career pathways of academic women. *Change: The Magazine of Higher Learning, 47*(2), 6–12. Retrieved from http://hostos.ezproxy.cuny.edu:2048/login?url=http://search.ebscohost.com/login.aspx?direct=true&db=eric&AN=EJ1057047&site=ehost-live

Harley, D., Acord, S. K., Earl-Novell, S., Lawrence, S., & King, C. J. (2010, January). Assessing the future landscape of scholarly communication: An exploration of faculty values and needs in seven disciplines. *Center for Studies in Higher Education, University of California/Berkeley.* Retrieved from http://escholarship.org/uc/cshe_fsc

Kinicki, A., & Fugate, M. (2018). *Organizational behavior: A practical problem-solving approach.* New York: McGraw-Hill.

Lynch, C. C., & Carleton, D. E. (2012). Lecture: Impact of digital scholarship on research libraries. *Journal of Library Administration, 52*(6–7), 456–473. https://doi.org/10.1080/01930826.2012.707947.

Professional Staff Congress of The City University of New York (PSC CUNY). (2015). *Constitution*. Retrieved from https://www.psc-cuny.org/about-us/constitution

Schein, E. H. (1999). Kurt Lewin's change theory in the field and in the classroom: Notes toward a model of managed learning. *Reflections, 1*(1), 59–74.

SECTION IV

"I only work with the converted": Converting the Technology Skeptics Through Proof and Credibility

CHAPTER 14

Living with the Skeptics: A Personal Journey

Sandy Figueroa

In 1995, why did I want to teach online when hardly anyone was teaching online? What resonated with me in 1995 that still resonates with me about online teaching? That year, the director of the Academic Computing Center offered a professional development workshop on how to use something called Web Course in a Box in our teaching. That workshop sparked my decades-long foray into online teaching. Web Course in a Box was the precursor to the sophisticated Learning Management Systems we see today. Even then, before the explosion in social media, mobile devices, or even graphical web browsers, I was curious about online teaching and learning. What were the possibilities for better teaching in an online environment over face-to-face teaching? How would the students react? After all, both they and I were used to the traditional teaching methods of lecture and group work. Would the students be able to learn the material better at their own pace in an online environment? After taking the professional development workshop on Web Course in a Box, I wanted to learn more about and become more proficient with online teaching and learning. Through online teaching, as rudimentary as Web Course in a Box was back in 1995, I saw the potential to reach a larger number of students and

S. Figueroa (✉)
Business Department, Hostos Community College, CUNY, Bronx, NY, USA
e-mail: sfigueroa@hostos.cuny.edu

to interact with more than just the ones who always answered in class. It meant a lot to me that in the online environment every student had to participate in the class discussion and assignments. The fact that the students could not just drift while listening to a lecture or hide behind a team member in a group project encouraged me to pursue online teaching.

When I mentor a faculty member who wants to take the plunge and teach online, I invite the faculty member to my office to just sit and talk about teaching in general and about teaching online in particular. Effective online teaching begins with the questions: Why do you want to teach online? What is there about online teaching that you cannot do face-to-face? Before any talk of pedagogy or attempt to learn the technology, the discussion has to center on the reason for venturing into online teaching or really any new pedagogy. The reason drives the exploration.

Technology has always been a major part of my teaching. As a high school Gregg shorthand and typing teacher, I had to incorporate different methods of teaching in order to be successful. At the time, the typewriter was the technology I had to use to teach my students to type. As an undergraduate and graduate student at Hunter College (CUNY) from 1967 to 1975, I was required to incorporate audio visuals in the lesson plans in our methods courses of teaching shorthand and typing. We had to develop lesson plans using the overhead projector, the opaque projector, 35 mm to create slides, and music. Each lesson had to incorporate one of these technologies in it. In addition, we had to present these lesson plans to the students in our methods courses for their feedback as well as the feedback from the instructor. I developed brief-form slides so that the students could identify the Gregg shorthand brief-forms and write them as quickly as possible in a 30-second time frame. I wrote the shorthand principles on the overhead projector, and I used music in the typing class to coordinate the students' finger movement with the music so that they were conscious of the words they were typing. By the end of the semester in our methods courses, we had lesson plans in which all three of the technologies were used. These technologies had to be incorporated at various points in our lesson plans. Becoming proficient in all of these techniques was essential in my field of teaching secretarial subjects.

I also taught high school general business and required the students to make a radio commercial. In the early and mid-1970s, students did not have access to cell phones with built-in cameras or even basic video cameras to create their own videos. The students made audio commercials and, with the help of the high school librarian, I was able to make a video of the students' commercials.

In my teaching prior to online teaching, I used an overhead projector in the Beginning and Advanced shorthand classes as well as my typing class. I continued to use the brief-form filmstrips that I created in my graduate methods course for teaching shorthand. In my typing classes, I continued to use music to synchronize their pacing for accuracy and speed in typing. Definitely the use of instructional technology, even then, was prominent in my teaching and showed me that I could do a lot more with my lessons through the use of audio-visual equipment.

By the time I came to Hostos in 1979, shorthand was on its way out. In the late 1980s, I was teaching computer-literacy classes and more advanced computer courses. By the mid-1990s, there was talk of online teaching, and that is when I began to learn about online teaching through the professional development workshops.

Blackboard bought *Web Course in a Box* and a number of other platforms. CUNY then received a grant from Sloan Kettering to invite faculty to develop asynchronous online-courses through the use of Blackboard, and the rest, as the expression goes, is history. Online teaching was a natural extension of the use of media in my teaching. With asynchronous online teaching, I knew that I could expand the walls of the classroom and reach more students because I had more contact with them on an individual basis; and the students could learn on their own with me as their guide. In addition, through the same grant, CUNY was able to offer faculty development for teaching writing-intensive courses in an online environment. Eager to perfect my online teaching, I enrolled in all of the online faculty-development workshops.

With my first foray into online teaching back in 1996, I learned the tools that were available in Blackboard at the time. Online teaching back then took the form of mainly posting syllabi and assignments on Blackboard as well as downloading papers, correcting papers, and uploading the corrected assignments. The Discussion Board was the main tool for students to use to interact with the faculty and each other. The online experience back then was limited. However, I did notice a vast difference in student participation and accountability. Most of the students in the online classes completed their assignments on time and with greater accuracy. The feeling of connectedness with the students was stronger and more exciting. For two semesters, I had the online students form teams and work on team projects. The team work was very good in those two semesters.

However, for the third semester, I had to abandon the idea of teamwork because the students were definitely not ready to work in teams online.

As the Blackboard tools for interaction became more sophisticated, I was able to *meet* students online, use Wikis more effectively, and move students to interact more with each other through the discussion board and their team Wikis. Now I can even revisit the formation of groups and the creation of group projects with these new and better interactive tools.

Serving as a mentor with the Online Initiative helped me to examine my own online practices and learn new techniques from other seasoned online faculty.

Notice that I do not solicit a faculty member to teach online. There is a great deal of information disseminated in the college to encourage faculty to teach online. Once a faculty member expresses an interest and asks me to be a mentor, that is when we talk. There are some departments that do not encourage the faculty to teach online, regardless of the faculty member's desire to engage in the pedagogy. When the individual asks for my advice, I simply suggest to the faculty member to ask the chair of the departmental curriculum committee to make a presentation on the importance, use, and significance of online teaching and learning. If the department chair and/or curriculum committee is unwilling to encourage the faculty member to teach online, the latter does have recourse to seek assistance outside the department. However, I would encourage that action only if the faculty member has tenure.

In the twenty-first century, our students are experiencing rapid technological changes that are far different from those of us who are *digital immigrants*, and technological advances will continue way beyond the twenty-first century. In actuality, we have all been using technology since our birth. The difference is that the information that we are receiving is coming to us faster than the traditional media of television and radio. I ask faculty who come to me for advice about teaching online if they are comfortable with a method in which they talk for the entire class period with occasionally one or two students answering or asking questions in class.

Students are coming to the college classroom with the experience of using the Internet in their junior and senior high school classes. They utilize their smartphones as their device of choice and can perform almost the same activities as they can on a computer or laptop. As can be seen through the Hostos Online Learning Assessment project, more and more students enroll in hybrid or asynchronous courses. How much longer will it take for department chairs and departmental curriculum committees to see that students are eager to learn online, whether hybrid or asynchronous? Most of the research in online teaching show that there is no significant difference in learning the material more effectively whether online or face-to-face. That being the case, since we are not hurting the students with online teaching, how long will it take the faculty to see that enrollment will drop in their traditional, in-person courses?

Faculty who are unsure about treading the waters of online teaching are not skeptics. They are pioneers in their discipline who want to make sure that they are successful in the new methodology, which by now is dated. The skeptics are the ones who refuse to recognize the value of online teaching and learning and limit themselves to the tried and true methods of teaching and learning. I work only with the converted. I leave the proselytizing to those who have the patience to convince others to join the movement for more research and dissemination of best practices for online teaching and learning. Online teaching is an opportunity for growth, exploration, and learning for both the teacher and the student. We are all researching and scratching the surface of the potential and power of online teaching and learning.

CHAPTER 15

Connecting the Dots: Data from a Personal Perspective

Kate S. Wolfe

Professor Sandy Figueroa and I came to online teaching in very different ways. It makes sense that someone who teaches Office Technology in the Business department would be an early adopter of online teaching. For me it took longer; I was educated in a Liberal Arts Psychology major at a large undergraduate institution and then at a large graduate institution, both in Texas. Technology was not a part of my education, except for data-analytic tools. As a graduate-teaching assistant I used grading programs, but that was the extent of my technology education.

I came to Hostos Community College as a new hire in 2012, with experience in teaching online. I was not an early adopter, but I started teaching online out of necessity as my life was changing in unexpected ways. I was teaching at a college in Washington State, where I had begun teaching online, and was trained using an online-training course for the Angel learning-management system. In 2010, my wife was accepted into an elite women's college in Massachusetts. I struck a bargain with my interim dean to let me teach online full-time from Massachusetts for one

K. S. Wolfe (✉)
Behavioral and Social Sciences Department, Hostos Community College, CUNY, Bronx, NY, USA
e-mail: kwolfe@hostos.cuny.edu

© The Author(s) 2019
K. S. Wolfe et al. (eds.), *Developing Educational Technology at an Urban Community College*, https://doi.org/10.1007/978-3-030-17038-7_15

year so that I could accompany her to Massachusetts. This was extraordinary as, in my opinion, many administrators want to see you on campus, and if they do not see you, I believe some think you are not doing your job. I taught my full teaching load online for one year (three academic quarters) from a great distance. I came back twice for some meetings and student get-togethers. At the end of the year, my new dean told me to return to Washington State. I then decided to resign. During this year I was also teaching part-time at colleges in Massachusetts and Connecticut, which gave me back-up. I became solely an adjunct at these colleges in 2011. At one of these colleges, I taught several courses online using the Moodle learning-management system. These experiences helped me learn a lot about online teaching and learning.

As a Psychology professor in the department of Behavioral and Social Sciences, I have had many opportunities to further my professional development and further my tenure and promotion efforts. I was immediately assigned to create a hybrid Social Psychology course so I joined the hybrid-initiative trainings offered by EdTech. I had taught this course many times as this was my field. I had to genuinely think about the time I spent with my students and what I wanted to accomplish. I wanted students to think more deeply about our topics so I expected readings to be done outside of class, and then we would have a mixture of lectures, class activities, reading quizzes, discussions, and videos in our face-to-face meetings. After that, I signed up every semester to develop either an asynchronous or a hybrid course. I now teach many Psychology courses as hybrids and three online.

Working with EdTech every semester gave me insights into their perspectives and helped me bond with their team members. In 2015, Carlos Guevara, the director of EdTech wanted to create a committee devoted to online research and asked me to come on board as coordinator (with release-time) of the Hostos Online Learning Assessment (HOLA) Task Force. That summer I submitted the Institutional Review Board (IRB) application necessary for research with human subjects. After some revisions engaged in by the entire HOLA team, our application for the HOLA Student Perceptions of Online Learning Survey was approved. Since then we have gathered student surveys every semester for two years; we changed to annual surveys in 2019 as we are expanding our focus to study faculty perceptions of online learning as well. We will now, therefore, be giving the student surveys in the spring semesters and the faculty surveys in the fall semesters. In 2018, Professor Kate Lyons and Dr. Kristopher Burrell took over (with release-time) as coordinators of the HOLA Task Force, with Burrell being the principal investigator for the faculty-perceptions survey. At this point I took over leadership of the Educational Technology & Leadership Council (ETLC) (with release-time) from Lyons. All three faculty liaisons work closely with Guevara; we have bi-weekly meetings to discuss the ETLC, HOLA, both surveys, presentation plans, and publication plans. Thus far, two articles have been published in the *Hispanic Education and Technology Services Online Journal* (see Chap. 3 in this section for a list of HOLA presentations and publications). All of our efforts are collaborative; therefore, this applies to all faculty involved in the HOLA task force, past and present.

I was recently inspired by one of our ETLC members at the Innovation Celebration in December 2018 to try game-based learning in my classes in the upcoming semester. Professor Juno Morrow demonstrated Kahoot!—an application for a smartphone as well as an Internet-based game. Faculty can create games on the spot for a class the same day. I had the opportunity to play one of these at the Innovation Celebration and saw how engaged the faculty, staff, and administrators became as the game progressed. People were very competitive, and it was fun! I would like to encourage some healthy competition as I have seen before how much it aids in student engagement. I hope that my students this semester will be engaged and motivated to read by the use of this game in my Psychology courses.

Nothing could be accomplished here without collaboration, cooperation, and the values espoused by EdTech that involve risk-taking, community building, and innovation. The HOLA and EdTech teams have much overlap, and we all work well together. I have never seen such a well-organized Educational Technology department with the outreach efforts that help encourage faculty to become adopters, no matter the point of the adoption curve at which they see themselves. My research background as a social psychologist has been helpful in designing the student-perceptions study and requisite IRB, and also in informing the faculty survey research study. I value the knowledge I have gained working with this team as well as the collegiality and friendships that have developed. I look forward to continuing my work as ETLC chair and on the faculty-perceptions and student-perceptions research. ETLC and HOLA have been a large part of my Hostos experience. I often feel lucky that I came along just at the right time and I benefited from the experiences of the early adopters like Figueroa and DiSanto.

CHAPTER 16

Building Community Through Assessment

Kate S. Wolfe and Jacqueline M. DiSanto

This chapter describes the Hostos Online Learning Assessment (HOLA) project: what it is and why it is important for encouraging technology adoption, change, and community building.

THE BEGINNINGS OF HOLA

According to their website, the Office of Educational Technology (EdTech) at Hostos Community College "develops, implements, supports, and promotes innovative integration of technology into teaching and learning by empowering faculty, serving students, and creating a supportive environment for all types of learners" (HCC EdTech, 2018a). Two of the five critical points outlined on its webpage specifically address the main participants in online education—the students and the faculty. EdTech assists "faculty in the integration of technology in their pedagogical models" and supports "students in the acquisition of technology skills"

K. S. Wolfe (✉)
Behavioral and Social Sciences Department, Hostos Community College, CUNY, Bronx, NY, USA
e-mail: kwolfe@hostos.cuny.edu

J. M. DiSanto
Education Department, Hostos Community College, CUNY, Bronx, NY, USA
e-mail: jdisanto@hostos.cuny.edu

© The Author(s) 2019
K. S. Wolfe et al. (eds.), *Developing Educational Technology at an Urban Community College*, https://doi.org/10.1007/978-3-030-17038-7_16

(2018a). The big question, though, addressed both students and faculty is this: do we know if what we are providing is working, is enough, or is even reaching the people for which it was intended?

Chairs and coordinators responsible for creating schedules, a role that includes determining how many online sections should be offered each semester, were faced with making a decision without any supporting reasons for selecting a specific number. Assumptions could be made that more or less students preferred learning online, but did we ever get it right? Advisors could offer reassurances to students that they would face the same level of academic challenge in an online section compared with what they experience in a face-to-face setting, but without research, the statement would be assumptive.

EdTech, whose third and fifth critical points are, respectively, to forge "partnerships in the research and development of educational technologies" and to build "partnerships across disciplines and departments" (HCC/EdTech, 2018a), sought to do just that in an effort to be able to provide concrete information to those involved in any way with online education and to be able to provide effective training and support for students and teachers in those courses. By purposefully bringing faculty from across the different academic content areas but who shared a dedication to online learning, specifically as a research project, EdTech began an introspective look into the different attitudes toward, preparedness for, experiences in, and reasons for being in an online class.

The Hostos Online Learning Assessment (HOLA) Task Force formally began in the academic year 2014–2015. As part of his vision to establish a solid framework for expanding online learning at Hostos Community College, Carlos Guevara, director of EdTech, decided to form a task force to support the fulfillment of the mission and strategic goals of the office, and build a process of continuous improvement for online learning. The committee consisted of full-time faculty from the Behavioral and Social Sciences (Kristopher Burrell, Sarah Hoiland, and Kate Wolfe), Business (Sandy Figueroa and Linda Ridley), Education (Jacqueline DiSanto), and Library (Kate Lyons) departments, and EdTech staff (Aaron Davis, Carlos Guevara, Iber Poma, and Wilfredo Rodriguez). Wolfe assumed the role of HOLA coordinator and faculty liaison to EdTech in 2015; she had participated in these initiatives since joining the Hostos faculty in August 2012. The task force began having discussions as a natural outgrowth of the Hostos asynchronous and hybrid initiatives, which provided all involved faculty an opportunity to meet the EdTech staff and become familiar with the policies and procedures at our institution. Participation in these online-learning initiatives was key to understanding how to develop and teach a variety of courses. The initiatives also served as a means to raise questions about what preconceived ideas students might have about online learning, how the students perceived their online experiences, and, even, whether the students know that class had started. These questions led to research conducted by the HOLA Task Force, which has informed changes made in the online initiative (faculty training).

Among the questions raised by this group were whether or not students were fully aware that they had indeed registered in an online course, and if they deliberately chose this format, what were their reasons for doing so. Once in the online section, how easily students accessed the course, from what location and type of device, and whether or not this access was adequate were also of interest. Additionally, the task force was interested in learning about communication between student and instructor, as well as among students, and the students' self-awareness about how they were doing in the course. The group spent much time deliberating on the spirit of each question, ascertaining exactly what were they seeking to learn, and on rewording it, so as to eliminate bias and ambiguity.

The team created a pilot survey that was administered to students enrolled in an online section. The college currently offers two types of online courses—hybrid and asynchronous. To be considered a hybrid course, 30% or more of a course's content must be offered online, with at least a third of the meetings taking place face-to-face. An asynchronous designation means that at least 80% needs to be offered online (HCC EdTech, 2018b). Out of 1270 total sections offered in fall 2015, approximately 4% of courses (59 course sections) were offered in the hybrid modality and 2% (29 courses sections) were offered in the asynchronous modality.

In the spring of 2015, a 23-question pilot survey was distributed, and 161 students responded. The authors met during the summer of 2015 in order to analyze the data and to discuss whether revisions needed to be made to the survey; as a group, they decided that greater specificity was needed with a more streamlined survey experience for students. In order to collect data formally, the authors obtained human-subject research approval from the college's Human Research Protection Program (HRPP, formerly known as Internal Review Board [IRB]) in September 2015. Hoiland and Wolfe then worked on making the amendments to the pilot survey created by the team. A formal research project was presented to

HRPP/IRB, which received full approval in fall 2015 for 2015–2019 (see Appendix 1). This approval allowed the team to conduct research, disseminate findings at conferences, and publish articles. Results from this survey are also used to improve the support and services provided for online learning at Hostos.

The HOLA Task Force developed the following three hypotheses: (1) students would indicate that their experiences in online courses is comparable to their experiences in face-to-face courses (in terms of workload, level of course difficulty, and engagement with both the instructor and other students in the course); (2) students would access the course from multiple devices and multiple locations; (3) students would indicate ease in navigating their hybrid and asynchronous courses. In addition, we examined the responses to questions that were not directly related to the hypotheses.

The initial survey had a response rate of 10% of online students, enrolled in asynchronous and hybrid courses. No incentives were provided for students to complete the survey, and all responses were anonymous. Faculty were emailed the background information on the survey and asked to request their students to complete the survey by the closing date. Additional reminders were sent to faculty via email and in-person at meetings.

For our first hypothesis, we found that the majority of students (60%) perceived online courses to be similar to face-to-face courses in terms of level of difficulty contradicting other literature that demonstrates that students perceive online courses to be easier (Jaggars, 2014). This could be explained by this student population, which is disproportionately remedial in comparison to other community colleges. Additionally, the high number of English-language learners and students who speak a language other than English at home and the number of students with work and family responsibilities that limit their ability to be on campus may result in fewer students perceiving any course as "less difficult" than others.

Hypothesis 2 was also confirmed. Our data shows that students access their online course from multiple devices and in multiple locations. Given the tremendous capabilities of smartphones and laptops, it makes sense that the vast majority (90%) of respondents believed they had adequate access to technology; however, our survey did not specifically address issues of Internet connectivity nor did it address which devices students have access to during quizzes and exams. We also did not ask the students to specify the amount of time they spent using the Internet when not in class. Learning how many students may not be proficient in manipulating the Internet could help the instructor be proactive by perhaps including short videos on how to do different online tasks such as using the library database for research. More specific questions such as "Did you ever lose your Internet connection during a quiz or exam?" would be helpful as would "How many people share the main device you use for the online class?"

Several students made comments in the qualitative section to the effect that the Blackboard App was not particularly useful (thus making it difficult to complete work on their phones) and/or that Blackboard posed technical problems as a course-management system. Members of the HOLA Task Force have indicated that students reported losing their Internet signal during a quiz or exam, and many others use their cell phone for lengthy written responses on journals, blogs, Wikis, and discussion forums, and also on quizzes and exams. Thus, students may have access to multiple devices but lack the appropriate device and/or stable Internet connection to succeed on a particular task (see Chap. 5). With respect to students accessing the course from multiple devices and multiple locations, the majority accessed their online classes via their personal laptop from home. The HOLA Task Force decided it needed to seek more specific data in terms of which devices were being used for what tasks and in which places were the students most likely to complete coursework. This would illuminate some of the lingering questions related to Internet access and the limitations of cellular devices with specific Blackboard features such as quizzes and exams.

For the last hypothesis, the findings suggest that students perceived that they generally navigated the Blackboard course site fairly well and that qualitative feedback about current instructors was very positive; however, many students wrote lengthy responses about course design when asked about Blackboard features. They also referenced poor course design in their previous online courses. Thus, targeted professional development for faculty who have been teaching online for several years was recommended to help them update their course design. This coincides with larger studies of online learning that show course design is one of the most important aspects of student performance in the online environment (Jaggars & Bailey, 2010).

The results of this study have been presented at several conferences, including HETS Best Practices Showcase in San Juan, Puerto Rico, CUNY IT Conference, Bronx EdTech Showcase, and CUE Conference. They have also been shared with the broader professional community.

The HOLA Task Force published two articles about this research in the *Hispanic Educational Technology Services (HETS) Online Journal*. In spring 2016, all HOLA Task Force members co-authored "Hostos Online Learning Assessment: A Survey of Student Perceptions", which discussed the group's initial findings (Wolfe et al., 2016). After this joint effort, the task force purposefully decided to work in smaller groups on different projects. *HETS* also published their second article, "Hostos Online Learning Assessment (HOLA) Follow-up: Student Perceptions in Two Cohorts" (Wolfe, DiSanto, Poma, & Rodriguez, 2018), which compared the findings of two administrations of the survey.

The survey was revised in spring 2016, an amendment was submitted to CUNY's HRPP/IRB process, and we received approval to use the new survey in spring 2016 (See Appendix 2). The HOLA Task Force plans to examine the data collected from three cohorts using this survey in fall 2018.

Future plans include focusing on outreach to increase student participation and further revision of the survey when the HRPP/IRB approval expires in 2019. The current survey does not separate out students in hybrid and asynchronous courses, but the task force would like to assess any differences in student perceptions as a function of online modality.

HOLA's Mission

The task force drafted a mission statement in fall 2017 that reads:

> The Hostos Online Learning Assessment (HOLA) Task Force has been established for three main purposes: to evaluate the effectiveness of the resources the college provides to support faculty and students engaged in hybrid and asynchronous teaching and learning; to investigate student perceptions about their learning experiences matriculating through hybrid and asynchronous courses; and to investigate faculty perceptions about the benefits and potential drawbacks of hybrid and asynchronous teaching.
>
> The HOLA Task Force endeavors to research the activities at Hostos Community College related to hybrid and asynchronous teaching and learning, in order to improve the experiences of faculty members and students at the college. The HOLA Task Force seeks to collect and provide empirical data that will educate the Hostos community about the current state of hybrid and asynchronous education at the college.
>
> The HOLA Task Force also seeks to disseminate its findings beyond the college, contributing to the scholarship of online teaching and learning. The

HOLA Task Force will also solicit and propose ideas that could potentially improve training methods for faculty interested in online teaching, increase the accessibility of technological resources for faculty and students, and raise the quality of student education in the hybrid and online learning environments.

Furthermore, the task force is appreciative of the need for collegiality and shared expertise when working on critical research and publishing projects, particularly over long periods of time, in order to maintain engagement (Eib & Miller, 2006). The HOLA Task Force serves as a self-contained faculty-development network with all members remaining actively committed to and involved in online teaching, while individually contributing technological skills, the ability to script surveys, and expertise in data analysis.

Current Activities

HOLA Student Surveys

The HOLA Task Force began the student perceptions of online-learning survey with a pilot in 2015. After receiving approval from CUNY's HRPP/IRB, the survey began to be administered for research purposes in the fall of 2015. The HOLA Task Force continues to examine student perception of online learning, which now includes comparing data between cohorts to identify changes and/or trends within the responses. As the approval expires in 2019, the task force has begun re-examining the survey in order to be ready to submit a new IRB application for the continuation of this research. The team plans to conduct the student survey annually, every spring.

Comparison of Findings

As data is collected from the different cohorts, there exists a wealth of information to be considered, especially as the team applies for IRB renewal and addresses the possibility of reframing existing questions or adding additional ones. For example, when writing the second of the published articles, which compared the results from two cohorts, the team raised the question of whether or not increasing awareness of online courses, particularly for students who had been new to this format and were now taking an online course for perhaps the second or third semester could impact their responses. An additional point of curiosity was to discuss whether or not to change the design of the survey to remove any chance of the survey becoming routine for students responding to every year.

Development of HOLA Faculty-Perceptions Survey

Faculty liaison Burrell spearheaded the creation of the 17-item Faculty-Perceptions Survey, along with a small team that included DiSanto, Figueroa, and Wolfe, in spring 2018 (see Appendix 3). This survey was submitted to CUNY's HRPP/IRB process and was approved for administration to faculty of asynchronous and hybrid courses in fall 2018. The plan is for the Faculty-Perception Survey to be given to online faculty annually during the fall semester. This will allow the team to begin examining faculty perceptions of their training to teach online and of their actual teaching of online courses.

Creating and inviting colleagues to complete this survey will in itself serve to support the community of online-learning participants, as it will offer them a chance to be heard and to have the experiences of those actively engaged in asynchronous and hybrid education count in future activities. It will give EdTech the opportunity to use hard data gleaned directly from the campus as the basis for assessing the effectiveness of its training initiatives as opposed to solely considering national trends or proclaimed best practices.

Assess EdTech Training of Online Faculty

One outcome of the Faculty-Perceptions Survey is to learn first-hand how relevant the training for online faculty was and how smoothly they were able to transition from participant in the initiative to provider of instruction in the online course. Resultant findings from this survey will be shared with EdTech, which is the driving force behind the asynchronous and hybrid initiatives. With very few exceptions, all instructors teaching in an online environment receive their training through this mentored training and have their online sections deemed acceptable before they can actually be assigned to teach that section. To learn what faculty already actively teaching online have to say about their training and implementation of this preparation could help further refine the initiatives and help recruit new faculty to teach online at our campus.

EdTech needs to know what is effective and what needs improvement in the training of faculty enrolled in the asynchronous and hybrid initiatives for online teaching effectiveness. The HOLA Task force needs to determine if faculty actually continue to teach online after completing training through one of the initiatives and, if they do, to identify what are their continuing faculty-development needs. If the faculty do not continue teaching online, it is important to know why and then determine what changes are needed to encourage faculty to continue teaching online. It is also important that the online faculty have an opportunity to assess their training after putting it to practical use.

HOLA Members

EdTech Staff

Carlos Guevara (director) has been part of the Office of Educational Technology since its inception in 2002, and under his leadership, this and a number of initiatives have been instituted to successfully contribute to promote an organizational culture change at Hostos during this decade. The HOLA Task Force is close to his heart as online learning is one of his areas of expertise and research interest, which have helped to provide guidance on the different horizons the task force has and will be embarking on.

Iber Poma (coordinator for student support) joined the Office of Educational Technology in 2004 and is in charge of the student support areas. Poma focuses on providing technology training to students, as well as support on a variety of academic technologies to enhance teaching and learning, and student experience in online learning environments.

Wilfredo Rodriguez (office coordinator) joined the Office of Educational Technology in 2012, coming to EdTech from the Office of Academic Affairs. Rodriguez is in charge of the day-to-day operations of the office, and focuses on faculty development, applications development and support, and outreach and creative work from instructional designers and design interns.

Faculty

Kristopher Burrell (chair, HOLA Task Force) had been an adjunct faculty before becoming an Assistant Professor of History in the Behavioral and Social Sciences Department in 2013. He joined the HOLA Task Force in the spring of 2015 when it began. He was asked to join because he had participated in the Hostos Hybrid/Asynchronous Initiative as a developer and mentor for multiple semesters. He felt it was important to be part of an initiative that might help improve the teaching of online and hybrid courses at Hostos. He believed that it was the role of faculty members on the task force to help develop ideas on how to disseminate the findings of the task force throughout the college. Faculty members need to candidly discuss how their teaching is going in their courses, what seems to be working well, and what challenges they are having. Faculty members need to use the information that we are gathering about student perceptions of online learning in order to make online and hybrid courses more accessible to and effective for students.

Jacqueline DiSanto is an Associate Professor in Early-Childhood Education with a background in faculty development and pedagogy. Her affinity for online learning began when she herself took eight of her required doctoral courses online. She joined this group in 2015 because of her own very positive experiences as the creator of several online sections and as a mentor to others, and also because she values the collegiality of the members and their appreciation of what both students and faculty have to say. This task force serves as an example for other programs and colleges, both within CUNY and outside our institution, because of its scholarly treatment of an innovative venue for delivering instruction. She believes that online instruction can be a contributing factor in improving retention and graduation rates at Hostos as it addresses multiple learning styles.

Sandy Figueroa is an Associate Professor in the Business Department and has vast experience teaching online. She joined the HOLA Task Force in 2015 because she wanted to work on making online teaching and learning successful for both learners and providers of instruction. She views the purpose of HOLA as to create, conduct, and facilitate research in online teaching and learning. She believes that the strength of the task force is that we have created a research project that we now have to disseminate among the faculty in the college. She sees dissemination as a key issue stating, "we deliver a product to the college community, CUNY, and, more broadly, academia" (personal communication, 2018).

Sarah Hoiland joined our faculty in 2013 as an Assistant Professor of Sociology in the Behavioral and Social Sciences Department. Later she joined the HOLA Task Force, in the beginning in Spring 2015, because she wanted to learn more about best practices in online teaching. She also wanted to be part of a team that was dedicated to online learning assessment. Her role has been that of a qualitative researcher. She helped create the student perceptions survey and used qualitative research software to analyze the written responses to open-ended qualitative questions related to student perceptions of online learning. Additionally, she thinks that the synergy created in a cross-disciplinary group of faculties combined with veteran professional staff members who are all passionate about the possibilities of teaching and learning online is the strength of the HOLA Task Force.

Kate Lyons (faculty EdTech liaison) joined the Educational Technology Department as a faculty liaison in 2008. She joined the HOLA Task Force at its inception. She wanted to work with the EdTech Office to encourage faculty to consider teaching online. She wanted to know whether online teaching is a good match for our faculty and staff at Hostos. It is necessary to gather data in order to convince people who are new to online learning that online teaching has good outcomes. On the other hand, if it is not a good fit, there needs to be a reevaluation of this goal of encouraging more online learning and a determination of why it is not working and what could be done to improve online teaching and training of online faculty.

Linda Ridley is a lecturer in the Business Department and joined the HOLA Task Force in 2015. She believes that the purpose of the HOLA Task Force is to build a culture of assessment in online learning at Hostos and to connect with other CUNY campuses to learn from others and to share our experiences. She also sees the importance of sharing our data with the larger Hostos community (administrators, faculty [both those who teach online and those who do not], and students).

Kate Wolfe (faculty, EdTech liaison; and chair, Educational Technology Leadership Council) joined the Hostos faculty in 2012 as an Assistant Professor of Psychology in the Behavioral and Social Sciences Department. She had previously taught online and immediately joined the Hybrid Initiative to develop a hybrid Psychology course. She currently teaches both hybrid and asynchronous courses. She joined Ed Tech as a faculty liaison in 2015. Her interests revolve around identifying effective pedagogy, the assessment of teaching and learning, and sharing best practices.

HOLA Task Force Conference Presentations

Burrell, K., Davis, A., DiSanto, J. M., Figueroa, S., Guevara, C., Hoiland, S., Lyons, K., Poma, I., Ridley, L., Rodriguez, W., & Wolfe, K. S. (2015, December). *Hostos Online Learning Assessment (HOLA) Project.* Presented at the CUNY IT Conference, John Jay College, New York, NY.

Hoiland, S., Wolfe, K. S., DiSanto, J. M., Burrell, K., Figueroa, S., & Ridley, L. (2016, May). *Hostos Online Learning Assessment: Utilizing student perceptions of online learning to improve online course delivery.* Presented at the Coordinated Undergraduate Education (CUE) Conference, Hostos Community College, Bronx, NY.

Wolfe, K. L., Burrell, K., DiSanto, J. M., & Ridley, L. (2016, May). Student perceptions of online earning at Hostos. Presented at the Bronx EdTech Showcase, Lehman College, Bronx, NY.

HOLA Task Force Publications

Wolfe, K. S., DiSanto, J. M., Poma, I., & Rodriguez, W. (2018). Hostos Online Learning Assessment (HOLA) Follow-up: Student perceptions in two cohorts. *Hispanic Educational Technology Services Online Journal, 8*(2), 19–51. Retrieved from https://hets.org/ejournal/2018/04/26/hostos-online-learning-assessment-hola-follow-up-student-perceptions-in-two-cohorts/

Wolfe, K. S., Hoiland, S. L., Lyons, K., Guevara, C., Burrell, K., DiSanto, J. M., Figueroa, S., Davis, A., Poma, I., Rodriguez, W., & Ridley, L. (2016). Hostos Online Learning Assessment: A survey of student perceptions. *Hispanic Educational Technology Services Online Journal, 6*(2). Retrieved from http://hets.org/ejournal/2016/04/28/hostos-online-learning-assessment-a-survey-of-student-perceptions/

Appendix 1

Hostos Online Learning Assessment Survey Fall 2015

To help plan future online courses and make improvements in this one, we would appreciate your feedback and suggestions. We want to learn from your experiences in and thoughts about this online course. Please take a few minutes to tell us what you think. Your responses will be kept anonymous. Thanks in advance for completing this survey.

1. **Did you realize you were signing up for a partially or fully online course when you registered?** *

   - Yes
   - No

2. **Which course are you in?** *

   - PSY 101
   - EDU 113
   - MAT 130
   - BUS 203
   - OT 104
   - BUS 100
   - HIS 210
   - SOC 101
   - ANT 101
   - Other:

3. **Tell us about your previous experience with online learning:** *
   Please check all that apply.

   - I've taken no other online courses.
   - I've taken hybrid courses at Hostos.
   - I've taken hybrid courses at another institution.
   - I've taken fully online courses at Hostos.
   - I've taken fully online courses at another institution.

4. **I registered for this course because:** *

   - Not Applicable—I didn't realize I was signing up for a partially or fully online course.
   - I live too far to attend an on-campus course.
   - I have a mental or physical disability that limits my ability to attend an on-campus course.
   - I was unable to find an on-campus section that would fit my class schedule.
   - All of the on-campus sections were full.
   - I needed extra units to be a full-time student.
   - I thought it would be easier than a face-to-face course.
   - I have work or family commitments that would not allow me to attend an on-campus course.

- There were no completely on-campus sections of this course.
- Other:

5. **How would you compare this online course to an on-campus course in the level of coursework difficulty?** *

   - This online course is more difficult.
   - This online course is at the same level of difficulty.
   - This online course is less difficult.

6. **How would you compare this online to an on-campus course in terms of the time you spent working on the course?** *

   - This online course involves more work.
   - This online course involves the same amount of work.
   - This online course involves less work.

7. **Do you feel like you have adequate access to technology in order to fully participate in this online course?** *

   - Yes
   - No

8. **I typically access this course on:** *
   Please check all that apply.

   - My personal desktop computer
   - My personal laptop
   - Hostos devices
   - Someone else's device
   - Cell phones
   - Tablets
   - Other:

9. **I typically access this course from:** *
   Please check all that apply.

   - Home
   - Work
   - Hostos Library
   - Hostos Open Lab
   - Other locations at Hostos
   - Other locations off-campus

10. **On the Blackboard site, it is easy for me to find:** *
    Please check all that apply.

    - The syllabus
    - Assignments
    - Exams
    - Policies
    - Discussion Boards
    - My grades
    - Contact info for the professor
    - Additional tools required for the course
    - Other:

11. **Compared to an in-person class, I feel as actively and enthusiastically engaged with the course and with the professor.** *

    - Strongly Agree
    - Agree
    - Disagree
    - Strongly Disagree
    - Not Applicable

12. **I communicate with the instructor using the following methods:** *
    Please check all that apply.

    - Email
    - In-person office hours
    - Skype or other online video chat software
    - Text messages
    - Phone
    - Other:

13. **I know how to find feedback about my progress in the course.** *

    - Strongly Agree
    - Agree
    - Disagree
    - Strongly Disagree
    - Not Applicable

14. **I interact with my peers in Blackboard in a timely manner (Discussions, Chat, Email, Comments).** *

    - Excellent
    - Above Average
    - Average
    - Below Average
    - Not Applicable

15. **I interact with my Instructor in Blackboard in a timely manner (Discussions, Chat, Email, Comments).** *

    - Excellent
    - Above Average
    - Average
    - Below Average
    - Not Applicable

16. **What are the most useful features of the online component of this course?** *
17. **Do you have any suggestions for improving the online component of this course?** *
18. **What other questions should we have included to get a better idea of the learning experience of this course?** *

Appendix 2

HOLA Student Perceptions of Online Learning Survey
Spring 2016

To help plan future online courses and make improvements in this one, we would appreciate your feedback and suggestions. We want to learn from your experiences in and thoughts about this online course. Please take a few minutes to tell us what you think. Your responses will be kept anonymous. Thanks in advance for completing this survey.

Did you realize you were signing up for a partially or fully online course when you registered?

- Yes
- No

I registered for this course because:

- Not Applicable (I didn't realize I was signing up for a partially or fully online course).
- I like to work independently.
- I prefer to choose when and where I will complete my course work.
- I was unable to find an on-campus section that would fit my class schedule.
- Of the instructor.
- I needed extra units to be a full-time student.
- I thought it would be easier than a face-to-face course.
- I have work or family commitments.
- There were no completely on-campus sections of this course.
- None of the above.

Tell us about your previous experience with online learning:
Please check all that apply.

- I've taken no other online courses.
- I've taken hybrid courses.
- I've taken fully online courses.

How would you compare this online course to an on-campus course in the level of coursework difficulty?

- This online course is more difficult.
- This online course is at the same level of difficulty.
- This online course is less difficult.

How would you compare this online course to an on-campus course in terms of the time you spent working on the course?

- This online course involves more work.
- This online course involves the same amount of work.
- This online course involves less work.

When I am completing my online coursework, I usually access the Internet using:

- Broadband/DSL
- My own secured wireless (Wi-fi) connection
- Public wireless (Wi-fi)
- My personal data plan
- I don't know

At some point in the semester, I lost my Internet connection while taking a timed quiz or exam.

- Yes
- No

I usually have access to a computer or tablet to complete my assignments and/or quizzes.

- Yes
- No

I access this course *on*:
Please check all that apply.

- My personal desk top computer
- My personal laptop
- Hostos devices
- Someone else's device
- Cell phones
- Tablets

I access this course *from*:
Please check all that apply.

- Home
- Work
- Hostos Library
- Hostos Computer Lab (ACC/C-595)
- Other

It is easy for me to find out when something is due.

- Strongly Agree
- Agree
- Disagree
- Strongly Disagree

It is easy for me to find out how to complete course requirements.

- Strongly Agree
- Agree
- Disagree
- Strongly Disagree

It is easy for me to find out my grade was and why I earned that grade on individual course requirements.

- Strongly Agree
- Agree
- Disagree
- Strongly Disagree

Compared to an in-person class, I feel as actively and enthusiastically engaged with the course and with the professor.

- Strongly Agree
- Agree
- Disagree
- Strongly Disagree

My instructor communicates with me (via Announcements, Discussion Forums, Blogs, Wikis, Collaborate, individualized feedback on required work, video, phone, and/or chat).

- Frequently (4+ times/week)
- Regularly (1–3 times/week)
- Sometimes (1 time/every 2 weeks)
- Rarely (1 time/month)
- Never

I interact with my peers in Blackboard (Discussion Forums, Blogs, Wikis, Collaborate, Chats).

- Frequently (4+ times/week)
- Regularly (1–3 times/week)
- Sometimes (1 time/every 2 weeks)
- Rarely (1 time/month)
- Never

I feel part of an online community.

- Strongly agree
- Agree
- Disagree
- Strongly disagree

What do you like best about online courses (please select one)?

- Flexibility and convenience (work, family, commute)
- More efficient use of time
- I can learn at my own pace
- I can teach myself
- Working alone

What do you like least about online courses (please select one)?

- Impersonal
- Lack of face time with instructors
- Lack of interaction with other students
- More work
- Too much self-discipline/responsibility needed
- Lack of instruction, lectures, and/or teaching
- I feel alone, isolated, and/or disconnected from the campus

Please select the word that describes you the best:

- Male
- Female
- Other

How old are you? _____
Are you a parent?

- Yes
- No

I speak a language other than English at home.

- Yes
- No

My last (or current) English class you have taken (or are taking) is:

- ESL 25
- ESL 35/36
- ESL 91/93
- ENG 101/102
- ENG 110/111

My background is:
- White
- Black
- Hispanic
- Asian/Pacific Islander
- American Indian/Alaskan Native
- Other/Unknown

I am the first person in my family to attend college.
- Yes
- No

Is there anything else you would like to share about your online learning experiences at Hostos in order to help us improve online education?

Appendix 3

Faculty Perceptions of Online Learning Survey

1. Please select your department (dropdown list of all departments)
2. What subject do you teach?
3. During the last academic year, how many hybrid course sections did you teach at Hostos?
   - More than 4
   - 3–4
   - 1–2
   - None
4. During the last academic year, how many asynchronous course sections did you teach at Hostos?
   - More than 4
   - 3–4
   - 1–2
   - None

5. What do you see as the benefits for your students in taking a partially or fully online course? (Check all that apply)
    - Convenience of location
    - Setting their own pace of learning
    - Saves students money (e.g. MetroCard, food, childcare)
    - Allows students to use their preferred learning styles
    - Accommodates work needs
    - Accommodates family responsibilities
    - Accommodates student preference to learn alone
    - Other

6. Based on your experience in your online courses, students have adequate access to technology overall.
    - Strongly Agree
    - Agree
    - Disagree
    - Strongly Disagree

7. Based on your experience in your online courses, students typically access this course on:
    - Their personal desktop computer
    - Their personal laptop
    - Hostos devices
    - Someone else's device
    - Cell phones
    - Tablets
    - Other:

8. Based on your experience in your online courses, students typically access this course from:
    - Home
    - Work
    - Hostos Library
    - Hostos Open Lab
    - Other locations at Hostos
    - Other locations off-campus
    - Other:

9. How difficult was it for you to develop the online (hybrid or asynchronous) courses you are currently teaching compared with preparing to teach a face-to-face course you had never taught before?

    - No difference in difficulty
    - Online version was less difficult
    - Online version was more difficult

10. How much time per week do you spend teaching the online (hybrid or asynchronous) courses you are currently teaching compared with teaching your face-to-face courses?

    - No difference in time
    - Less time spent on online course
    - More time spent on online course

11. How much time per week do you spend grading in the online (hybrid or asynchronous) courses you are currently teaching compared with grading in your face-to-face courses?

    - No difference in time
    - Less time spent on online course
    - More time spent on online course

12. I feel like I have adequate technology skills to teach online courses.

    - Strongly Agree
    - Agree
    - Disagree
    - Strongly Disagree

13. I have had adequate training to teach online courses.

    - Strongly Agree
    - Agree
    - Disagree
    - Strongly Disagree

14. Did you receive your training in online teaching?
15. List the 3 greatest obstacles for students who are enrolled in a partially or fully online course.

16. List the 3 greatest obstacles you experience when teaching a partially or fully online course.
17. What do you see as the benefits for you, as a faculty member, when you teach a partially or fully online course?

References

Eib, B. J., & Miller, P. (2006). Faculty development as community building. *International Review of Research in Open and Distance Learning, 2*(7), 1–15.

Hostos Community College Office of Educational Technology (HCC EdTech). (2018a). *Online course development for faculty*. Retrieved from https://commons.hostos.cuny.edu/online/faculty/

Hostos Community College Office of Educational Technology (HCC EdTech). (2018b). *Welcome to educational technology*. Retrieved from https://commons.hostos.cuny.edu/edtech/

Jaggars, S. (2014). Choosing between online and face-to-face courses: Community college student voices. *American Journal of Distance Education, 28*(1), 28–28. https://doi.org/10.1080/08923647.2014.867697.

Jaggars, S., & Bailey, R. (2010). *Effectiveness of fully online courses for college students: Response to a Department of Education meta-analysis*. Academic Commons, Columbia University. Retrieved from https://doi.org/10.7916/D85M63SM.

Wolfe, K., DiSanto, J. M., Poma, I., & Rodriguez, W. (2018). Hostos Online Learning Assessment (HOLA) follow-up: Student perceptions in two cohorts. *Hispanic Educational Technology Services Online Journal, 8*(2), 19–51. Retrieved from https://hets.org/ejournal/2018/04/26/hostos-online-learning-assessment-hola-follow-up-student-perceptions-in-two-cohorts/

Wolfe, K. S., Hoiland, S. L., Lyons, K., Guevara, C., Burrell, K. DiSanto, J. M., ... Ridley, L. (2016). Hostos Online Learning Assessment: A survey of student perceptions. *Hispanic Educational Technology Services Online Journal, 6*(2). Retrieved from http://hets.org/ejournal/2016/04/28/hostos-online-learning-assessment-a-survey-of-student-perceptions/

CHAPTER 17

Moving Through Hostos, a Student Grown into a Staff and Faculty Member

Rocio Rayo

On my first day, I nervously came in through the A building, slightly surprised that Public Safety let me in with just a quick flash of my ID. There appeared a daunting flight of stairs in front of me, and I began climbing. I reached the top, again surprised that no one had come running at me asking why I was there. Walking across the bridge, my posture straightened with the confidence that I had somehow been able to sneak by everyone without them knowing that maybe I did not belong. Once I crossed the bridge into the C building, I felt like I was officially playing the part of a college student. I was ready to continue this portrayal into my first class but when I went to the classroom, it was empty! Did I write the wrong room number down? Had my classroom changed? Maybe there was an email—but I couldn't check it on my phone. I panicked.

I went back to the bridge thinking that the library might be open and I hoped there were computers in there, but the library was closed. I walked back to the class to check again, but it was still dark and empty. I slowly trudged back to the bridge not knowing where to go or whom to ask for help. Feeling increasingly anxious, I looked up and saw a row of computers

R. Rayo (✉)
Hostos Community College, CUNY, Bronx, NY, USA
e-mail: RRayo@hostos.cuny.edu

© The Author(s) 2019
K. S. Wolfe et al. (eds.), *Developing Educational Technology at an Urban Community College*, https://doi.org/10.1007/978-3-030-17038-7_17

outside of the cafeteria! There was a Public-Safety officer standing by them; I tentatively asked him if I could use the computers, and he pointed to a sign above them that read "paid for through your technology fee" and said "that is what they are here for." I logged into my Hostos email and found that my professor had canceled class. This was my first experience with the supportive technology that Hostos, as an institution, offered its students.

My first semester was in 2009—before the "Obama phone" phenomena—and I had a Verizon flip phone and no-steady Wi-Fi connection at home. While this was also before Google Docs became a required component of a student's success, it meant that I had limited access to email, Blackboard, and any databases. This also meant that I spent a lot of time on campus. Like my first day of class, kiosks played a crucial role in my access to the staple of any Hostos student's life: their Hostos email. (This is tongue-in-cheek as it is always a struggle to get students to use their email!)

The library computers became my second gateway into cyberspace. I could not work at the kiosks. I needed to find a place that had a computer I could sit at and use. I happened upon the library computers one morning when I did not have a class but came to school anyway to do homework. I did not have any friends yet, so I walked around looking for a place to hide and read. I went to the computer lab first, but when I walked in I turned right around after looking at the sea of faces. I wandered over to the library thinking that, even if there weren't computers, I could read there. I walked downstairs and was happily greeted by computers! They were hidden away and were organized in small clusters—way less scary than the big computer lab. The added bonus was the printer didn't require me to walk in front of rows of strangers.

It did not take me long to make friends at Hostos. All my initial trepidation about being older, a mom, poor, and having failed before evaporated when I realized (a) my age meant experience I could apply to my classes; (b) I was not the only parent (c) poverty is systemic; (d) it wasn't about failing; it was about trying again. This meant that, when I wanted to study and work with friends, the library was no longer appropriate. I branched out to the computer lab. Walking in with a group felt empowering—I was part of a wave in the sea of faces rather than a single drop of water.

While I made many friends at Hostos, the most elemental in my continued success as a student came from the community of scholarship that I walked into by becoming part of the Honors Program. Computers and a printer located in the honors room directly facilitated this success. This room was reserved only for honors students. This was important for me as a parent who often had my son with me on the weekends and therefore could not go to the computer lab with my two-year-old. This was important for me as a student who did not have access to Wi-Fi at home and needed the Internet to complete assignments. The honors room was a place that was open whenever the college was open. It had a couch, four computers, and a printer. Most importantly the honors room was home to a group of students who embodied what it meant to be a successful Hostos student. We supported each other academically and emotionally.

In my second semester at Hostos, Rees Shad, one of my professors, asked me what I wanted to do when I "grew up." I told him I wanted to be a professor so I could inspire students the way he inspired me. Rees asked me if I knew what degrees I need to become a professor—at that point I had not thought about anything after Hostos, and I was still surprised I made it through my first semester. He helped me navigate the degrees and told me to go get my master's degree, then I could adjunct. So I did. In 2014—five years after my first semester at Hostos—I became a faculty member.

In my second semester teaching, I was assigned my first *smart* classroom. This meant that I had the opportunity to have a computer and a projector in the room. Prior to this I would outline my class lectures on index cards and write notes on the board. This was tedious, but felt natural since this was how most of the classes that I had taken operated. Once I was assigned a smart classroom, I transferred my index cards onto PowerPoint presentations to supplement my lectures. This felt like the obvious next step. It was a tremendous improvement to my lectures since I no longer had to spend time writing things out, but rather could just click through my learning outcomes. What I had not anticipated were the times in class where a discussion topic would come up that I had not included in my lecture and I had the opportunity to use the computer, Internet, and projector to incorporate multimedia in the classroom beyond PowerPoint presentations. Technology in the classroom also allowed me to assign multimedia presentations as a part of the student's coursework thereby giving students a chance to learn iMovie, Prezi, and/or PowerPoint.

Access to technology on campus provided a collaborative option for teaching as well. Many of my friends teach similar themes at other colleges around the country. Having access to their lectures, materials, and so on, gave me a bigger pool of resources to support my students. Using Blackboard as a platform for sharing resources created by the leading researchers in their field was an immensely important tool to be able to share with my students—for free.

I learned the pedagogical tool of flipping the classroom, at a National Science Foundation Conference in 2013. I was still in graduate school, but was co-teaching at the time with Prof. Shad. It appealed to me because it presented an opportunity to stray away from the standard lecture structured class into a discussion/workshop-based class without having to sacrifice the lecture. The lecture took place outside of the classroom on a communal learning platform, in our case: Blackboard. This changed the game for my teaching style. I was able to post PowerPoint presentations on Blackboard. I used assignments to track accountability. This resulted in classroom time being used for discussions, to incorporate critical thinking skills, and most importantly, to write together. Flipping the classroom aided my enormous responsibility as a professor to make sure my students leave as better writers than they were when they came into my class. Many of my students were not CUNY-proficient in writing, and the time that was created by flipping the classroom gave me an opportunity to help students work on their reading and writing skills together in a workshop-based setting.

After the initial excitement about the possibilities of flipping the classroom, I went home and told my mom about it. Her first question was, "What if people don't have a computer, or don't have Wi-Fi?" I paused—I didn't know the answer to that. I went back to work the next day and I asked around. What do we do? I overwhelmingly got the same answers that they all have phones or that they are always on the Internet. This, however, is a common false equivalency. Yes, many students at this time had phones, and, yes, many students often cruised on social media via the Internet. BUT that did not mean that their phones were conducive to engagement with online classroom material. In fact, in many cases it was the opposite. For example, Blackboard was initially extremely mobile *un*friendly. It has gotten better but it is still hard to navigate on a phone screen. Reading materials are often not mobile friendly. The tiny screen made it hard to navigate functions on Blackboard like quizzes or discussion boards, especially if it was the only way that the students were engaging with the Blackboard site.

The other challenge I faced with incorporating technology into my classroom was that, while the library and the computer lab were essential resources to students, the library is not open early in the morning or in the evening. The computer lab is seemingly always open; however, children are not allowed. Unfortunately not everyone had the opportunity to have the honors room as a resource like I had when I was student.

The community of scholarship that I found as an honors student was just as important as a professor. I found that community of scholarship again as a professor at the CTL's Spa Day, where I presented on a National Science Foundation grant I was working on with two other professors, Rees Shad and Catherine Lewis. We presented on an initiative entitled, "Game-Framed Math and Science." This was an initiative to address the remediation issue here at Hostos with Media-Design students—specifically, how to get students to be more comfortable with Math so that they are not stuck in remedial courses for semesters on end. Since Rees, Catherine, and I had all been together so closely—and it was my first project of this caliber—I had no context about the impact this type of project might have on the Hostos community. At our first presentation the room was full of folks who wanted to hear about our work—it was incredible.

Support systems are not only important to students. They are essential to faculty and staff. The EdTech and CTL community provided a physical meeting space for faculty to present our work, discuss the challenges we faced as well as the successes. The shared community of inquiry that emerges out of the CTL Spa Day and Bronx EdTech Showcase solidified my desire to continuing working on solutions for the particular issues that affect our Hostos Community via interdisciplinary channels. I had no idea all of the other initiatives that were happening simultaneously throughout the colleges targeted many of the same issues as our initiative. It was the first time I really understood the challenges that having silos of study created when attempting to solve an institutional problem.

The support systems—the social capital—that are built here become the roadmaps to success. The idea that silos, autonomous academic entities, will dissolve is impractical. The solution is not to deconstruct the silos; the solution is to deconstruct the power that those individual silos hold by creating systems of support between them. This is what educational technology did for me as a student, as a professor, and now as a staff member.

I look at the incoming class of first-year students this semester and I see excited faces. I see timid and shy faces, too. I see the faces of communities that I grew up in, that I live in—and I am proud. Hostos is made up of resilience. Resilience that doesn't come from birth but that comes from life. Hostos is a reflection of our South Bronx community, of our immigrant community, and of ourselves. Our technological practices are a reflection of that, too. We are innovators partly out of need, but mostly out of imagination. We have made things work with what we have, and we will continue.

Afterword

Kate Lyons, Carlos Guevara, and Kate S. Wolfe

Stocking and maintaining science labs, managing long and expensive commutes for members of a college campus, ensuring accessible classrooms—these are all examples of how the physical spaces associated with higher education are dependent on funding. Imagine if the costs of maintaining physical spaces for higher education were eliminated and all institutions, regardless of funding, could offer students more similar access to resources. In 2003, Linden Lab developed Second Life, a free virtual 3D world that gives users the freedom to build spaces that cross geographic boundaries and physical limits—where users can virtually learn, create art, and socialize with people they might not otherwise be able to meet in real life. Although brick-and-mortar universities began creating their virtual parallels in Second Life, it was Massive Open Online Courses (MOOCs) that were briefly heralded as game-changers for education. Taught using more traditional

K. Lyons
Hostos Community College, CUNY, Bronx, NY, USA

C. Guevara
Division of Academic Affairs, Hostos Community College, CUNY, Bronx, NY, USA

K. S. Wolfe
Department of Behavioral and Social Sciences, Hostos Community College, CUNY, Bronx, NY, USA

© The Author(s) 2019
K. S. Wolfe et al. (eds.), *Developing Educational Technology at an Urban Community College*, https://doi.org/10.1007/978-3-030-17038-7

learning-management systems, such as Blackboard, or by posting multimedia content to streaming sites like YouTube and Vimeo, these courses held the promise of access. Anyone, anywhere, regardless of their prior educational levels, could join MOOCs and advance in their fields, needing only the computing power available in most smart phones. Access to educational content online garnered much interest but ultimately did not come close to rendering traditional, in-person higher education obsolete. Although perceived as a game-changer, MOOCs failed to live up to the hype but have provided examples that can be used to improve higher education.

As of 2018, despite the gains in virtual and augmented reality, recently named mixed reality, and communications technology, we have yet to see a virtual, 3D parallel world, where educational institutions can set up shop, and instead of vying for digital leadership with each other, we can share our breakthroughs to enable all of us to reach higher levels of student success through richer learning environments. Although the 2D learning-management systems used today are not yet compelling enough for all students to choose online learning over in-person classes, the technology to realize 3D virtual spaces that more closely parallel reality remains on the horizon. Imagine that, as 2D learning-systems become immersive and 3D virtual-spaces live up to their potential, the inequalities presented by geographic boundaries could be leveled. Also imagine, if you will, the marked distinction between online and face-to-face learning is blurred, and faculty and students have the skills, equipment, and support to be more purposefully fluid when selecting their teaching and learning venues without having to consider what is more dependable or noteworthy. And do not forget to include the importance of data analysis and transparency to continue building the confidence of this community of innovators to identify the processes and systems that must change along with the implicit business culture and practice. Productivity and efficiency are important barometers to make better use of the limited resources we have.

Kate Lyons joined Hostos Community College in 2006, after working first as a web developer and then as a librarian with one of the largest digital-divide initiatives in a public library at that time, click on @ the library (New York Public Library [NYPL]). Lyons went from watching the tail end of the dot-com boom, with all the promise and gold rush-like appeal of a new frontier to explore, to watching those who missed the technology bubble. At NYPL Lyons saw firsthand how people without access to technology could not apply for jobs without the Internet and email, did not have the requisite skills for most jobs, could not access authoritative information in library databases, could not read the news for free, and paid extra by having to use travel agents and other services they could have readily replaced with websites.

Access to opportunities, access to technology, access to course content—access is a recurrent theme in this book. Chapter 4 describes Hostos students and the demographics in the South Bronx, and the stark contrast between their access to technology and those in the more affluent parts of New York City. Chapter 12 discusses the Open Educational Resources initiatives at Hostos, which sprang from the need to respond to students unable to purchase increasingly expensive commercial textbooks. The cost of education to students goes well beyond tuition. Supplies, commutes, course content, time—these costs can make education unattainable.

This book is about our experience with change management and organizational culture change—specifically our story about encouraging our campus community to adopt educational technology. As we met, discussed our experiences, read each other's chapters and reflections, it became clear that, for all of us, our success hinged on our shared devotion to the mission and also on the clear vision and trust we had purposefully built as a team.

In this book's foreword, our provost's words echo and reinforce the reason for our success—an organizational culture that values risk-taking and innovation. And by adopting this culture, we have given each other the space to trust that our colleagues will value our efforts. Ultimately, a clear vision and trust are the linchpin in our community. Without them, we could not engage in honest debate. We could not question authority or create new course content. We would not have the confidence to fail. Trust is where the book ends, because it is also the foundation upon which our vision will guide our work at Hostos.

Index

A
Academic Computing Center (ACC), 16, 53, 54, 163
Academic Works, 38, 141, 143, 155
  See also Institutional repository
Are You Ready? course, 45, 60, 92, 125–127, 129–133
Asynchronous guidelines, 87, 98, 130, 151

B
Badges, 31, 100, 105, 109, 110, 113–114, 116, 130
Bronx Community College (BCC), 5, 32, 58, 74, 75, 132, 139
Bronx EdTech Showcase, 59, 66, 68, 74–75, 100, 109, 132, 155–156, 177, 201
Burrell, Kristopher, 8, 16, 24, 58, 60, 170, 171, 174, 180, 181

C
Center for Teaching and Learning (CTL), vi, 12, 17, 88, 98, 101–103, 108, 109, 153, 201
Change agent, 4, 7, 9, 12, 16, 21, 26, 75
City University of New York (CUNY), v, 4–7, 13–15, 17, 24, 32, 35–37, 51–53, 55, 57–60, 66, 72, 74, 75, 87, 91, 96, 99, 100, 103, 107, 108, 125, 127, 132, 133, 138, 141, 143, 148, 149, 155, 157, 164, 165, 177–180, 182, 183
Committee on Academic Computing (CAC), 6
Committee on academic technology (CAT), 96, 98
Communal constructivism, 39–41
Community of practice (CoP), 6, 18, 75, 81, 95, 133
CTL, *see* Center for Teaching and Learning

INDEX

Cultural artifacts, 106, 110, 112
CUNY, *see* City University of New York

D
Diffusion of innovations theory, 7, 26, 28
Digital divide, 39, 40, 95, 204

E
EdTech faculty liaisons, 6, 8, 9, 24, 58, 174, 183
EdTech Innovations newsletter, 30
EdTech Leadership Council (ETLC), 17, 56, 57, 59, 66, 82, 84, 87, 92, 97–98, 107, 110, 112, 121, 150, 154, 171, 183
EdTech team
 faculty liaison, 4, 6–7, 9, 24
 formation of, 4
ePortfolios initiative, 71–73
ETLC, *see* EdTech Leadership Council

F
Flipping the classroom, 200

G
Gallardo, Julio, 53–55
Guevara, Carlos, 3–10, 22, 27, 28, 54, 57–60, 74, 75, 92, 96–98, 100–102, 106, 108, 127, 132, 151, 170, 171, 174, 181
Guidelines for reappointment, promotion and tenure, 148–150

H
HOLA, *see* Hostos Online Learning Assessment

Hostos Community College
 and the digital-divide, 204
 faculty demographics, 36–37
 library, 204
 mission, vi, 135, 144
 and social justice, 35
 student demographics, 36
Hostos Online Learning Assessment (HOLA), 31, 59, 91, 101, 116, 128, 133, 166, 170, 171, 173–184
Hybrid guidelines, 87, 98, 130, 151

I
Information Learning Commons Committee, 16
Innovation Celebration, 30–31, 100, 103, 105, 106, 108–116, 142, 171
Innovation Chase, 31, 100, 103, 105, 106, 109–111, 113, 114, 116, 142
Innovations Web
 community building node, 30
 continuous improvement node, 31
 dissemination and outreach node, 30
 ideas generator node, 28
 innovators recognition node, 31
 support structure node, 29
Institutional repository, 141–143, 155
iPad initiative, vi, 66–70

K
Kotter, John Paul, 9, 21, 116

L
Lecture Capture Initiative, 59, 69–71, 103
Lehman College, 5, 32, 58, 74, 75, 132
Lyons, Kate, 6–8, 16, 24, 58, 74, 75, 170, 171, 174, 183, 204

M

Mangino, Christine, 3, 17
Massive Open Online Courses (MOOCs), 3, 107, 108, 203, 204

O

Office of educational technology, 3, 5, 6, 10, 12, 17, 42, 56, 57, 65, 75, 80, 92, 95, 97, 125, 142, 147, 173, 181
  budget, 9
Office of Instructional Technology (OIT), vi, 14, 15, 54–56
Online learning
  assessment of, 133, 183 (*see also* HOLA)
  asynchronous courses, 4, 45, 46, 59, 60, 74, 76, 81, 82, 87, 89, 90, 96, 98, 120, 130, 132, 151, 165–167, 170, 175, 176, 178, 180, 181, 183, 195
  faculty perceptions of, 42–43, 116, 127, 128, 170
  hybrid courses, 4, 35, 45, 46, 59, 60, 74, 76, 81, 82, 87, 89, 90, 96, 98, 120, 128, 130, 132, 151, 166, 167, 170, 175, 176, 178, 180–183, 195
  and student engagement, 84
  student perceptions of, 101, 179, 182, 183 (*see also* HOLA)
  student preparedness (*see* Are you Ready? Course)
Online learning initiative
  and the mentoring experience, 46
  structure of, 83–84
  success of, 88–92
Open access, 136, 144, 145, 154, 155
Open Educational Resources (OERs), 92, 135–145, 205
  Achieving the Dream (AtD) grant, 138, 139
  5Rs, 136–137
  zero textbook cost degree, 141
Outreach, 8, 28, 30, 99–101, 155, 171, 178, 181

P

Pedagogy of the oppressed, 39, 40
Peer Observation Improvement Network for Teaching (POINT), 98, 151
Porte, Loreto, 14, 54, 150
Professional development, vi, 15, 18, 24, 27, 29–31, 42, 43, 65–76, 80, 88, 98, 101, 115, 119, 120, 151, 153, 163, 165, 170, 177
Professional Staff Congress (PSC), 148, 149

R

Risk-taking, 7, 8, 18, 23, 31, 32, 71, 102, 105, 106, 153, 158, 171, 205
Rogers, Everett, *see* Diffusion of Innovations

S

Sehgal, Varun, 58

T

Teaching Innovation Support Center (TISC), 54–56
Teaching observations, 150–152
Technology-adoption lifecycle, 80
Theory of learning organizations, 27

W

Wolfe, Kate, 8, 16, 24, 37, 42, 97, 100, 128, 174, 175, 178, 180, 183

Printed in the United States
By Bookmasters